WORDS OF PRAISE FOR GOD'S WORK THROUGH DAVE AND BETH CHILCOAT:

"Dave and Beth Chilcoat are two of my all time heroes. When Dave was diagnosed with Lou Gehrig's disease (ALS), he and Beth faced this debilitating and deadly disease with faith, courage, perseverance, and yes... humor. This is the story of their life together, and of Dave's death, as told through Dave's journal – a story no one will want to miss. Through it all, their relationship to Jesus Christ remained pre-eminent and was the reason for the grace with which they approached life and faced death. After reading this book, you sense the truth of the Apostle Paul's words, 'To live is Christ and to die is gain.'"

Denny Rydberg, President, Young Life

"...Woven into the story of Dave Chilcoat's battle with ALS are golden threads – Scripture, humor and tenacious love between a man and a woman... Wise people everywhere will treasure this guide. What Dave proclaimed to thousands in life, he experienced deeply in death and continues to share here: that the Gospel is the only hope for life, and death, and life again, forever."

Kelly Monroe Kullberg, author of *Finding God Beyond Harvard: the Quest for Veritas*, and Founder, the Veritas Forum

"Corrie ten Boom, a Christian prisoner in a Nazi death camp, once said, 'There is no hole so deep that God's love is not deeper still.' Dave Chilcoat's hole was the devastating impact of ALS that cut him down in the prime of his life. But this remarkable journal records Dave's discovery that Jesus' love is indeed deeper still. His profound insights are applicable to all of us who want to enjoy God's love in deeper ways."

Gary DeLashmutt, Lead Pastor at Xenos Christian Fellowship, Columbus, Ohio, and author of *Loving God's Way and Spiritual Relationships That Last*

Nobody Tells a Dying Guy to Shut Up

An Account of God's Faithfulness

from the online journal
of Dave Chilcoat
edited by Beth Chilcoat

ISBN: 978-0-9825676-0-9

Library of Congress Control Number: 2009938499

Printed in the United States of America

This book is printed on acid-free paper.

All Scripture quotations used in this book are listed in *Resources: Catalogue of Scripture References*. Scripture quotations marked Phillips come from J.B. Phillips: The New Testament for Modern English in Schools. Copyright © J.B. Phillips 1959, 1960. Used by permission of Geoffrey Bles Ltd. All rights reserved. Scripture quotations marked NIV are taken from the HOLY BIBLE, NEW INTERNATIONAL VERSION®. NIV®. Copyright©1973, 1978, 1984 by International Bible Society. Used by permission of Zondervan. All rights reserved. And those marked DCV come from the version of Scripture David Chilcoat kept in his heart.

While the author has made every effort to provide accurate Internet addresses at the time of publication, neither the publisher nor the author assumes any responsibility for errors, or for changes that occur after publication. Further, the publisher does not have any control over and does not assume any responsibility for author or third party websites or their content.

Book design by Gary Hoffman
Cover from Dave Chilcoat's well-used Bible

DEDICATION

To my beloved husband
who wrote his
love and acceptance
on every page of my life.

David Chilcoat
(1947 – 2006)

And to God
who led the journey
and blessed the journey
and is the Journey.

BC

Table of Contents

Acknowledgments

This book came about in much the same way as Columbus Young Life was birthed and Gideon fought the Midianites[1]: God brought it forth from nearly nothing since I am neither a writer nor an editor.

But He certainly supplied an abundance of material.

From the day he was diagnosed with ALS, my husband David kept a journal of his battle with the disease. It started in a personal diary. As word of his condition spread, family and friends clamored to know how he was doing. We were overwhelmed by their heart-felt interest. At the same time, David realized that God was using his situation to strengthen his faith, and give him new opportunities to proclaim Jesus' love. David began an online journal to share what God was teaching him and to keep people up to date on his physical con-dition. He was dying while he wrote it, so we paid little attention to editing. After three years of entries, it was huge!

Following David's death, many people encouraged me to share his story. As I prayed, it became clear I should let David speak for himself. I had no idea how to condense more than a thousand pages into a concise account of God's incredible faithfulness to us. Plus the grieving process is draining and, though I have always been motivated to get things done, my lethargy was intense. Merely reading David's words caused me pain.

Still, I believed God wanted me to publish David's journal for a wider audience. I asked Him to confirm that call, and clear what seemed to be three insurmountable obstacles:

It hurt to read the journal.

I did not have the skills.

I did not have a plan.

I prayed for a year and a half. Just as I was ready to give up, His answers began to come. For the pain, God brought two amazing sisters in Christ. Bev DeLashmutt, whom David had led to the Lord when she was a teen, passionately shared my belief that the journal should be published, and volunteered to come alongside me in the work. She brought her friend, Rosy Talarzyk, a widow who understands both suffering and joy in Jesus. Rosy did not even know David or me, but felt God's nudge to join us. Together we shared thousands of hours of prayer, work, laughter and tears. With them, this daunting process became a blessing of healing and fellowship; the pain did not go away, but it was shared, and that was enough.

As we read, edited, prayed and condensed, we began to understand what was needed and our skills improved. Each added unique gifts to the process, and the essence of David's journey and God's faithfulness began to emerge. We were amazed by the power of the message. But would others feel the same way?

Eight months into the project, we were invited to present David's perspective of joy in suffering at a national conference attended by more than a thousand pastors and church leaders. Now we really needed a plan in order to complete the book in time. Again we prayed for God's provision and leading for our task. Did He ever provide and lead!

We approached a talented, local author to read the manuscript and offer some advice. Kelly Monroe Kullberg did far more; she loved the journal and graciously joined us. Kelly brought with her an excellent editor, Carol Williams, and the team became five.

The five of us have been on such a faith journey! The generosity and dedication each of these talented women brought to the project leave me humbled and praising God. I will never be able to fully express how great a blessing it has been to share this process with them, and see Him graciously guide this adventure.

Whatever wisdom we needed, God has provided. Whatever

resources we lacked, He has more than met our needs. And I continue to learn to trust Him, although now without my beloved husband to encourage me, for God is faithful; He always does more, gives more. He promises that His power is made perfect in our weakness. I have had the great privilege of knowing that first hand.

Of course, there are many more to thank. When I first sat down to write these acknowledgments, I thought I could simply make a list of people who had touched and supported our family throughout the disease, my adjustment to life without David, and the creation of this book. But that list – all the people who ministered to us, fed us, prayed for us, took care of us, provided for us, helped us and loved us in countless ways – is enormous. To name everyone is impossible. I thank you for sharing God's love in such tangible ways. Truly you have been His gift to us and I praise Him for your generosity.

Thank you, also, to my precious family, who helped carry David and me through such hard times, and who continues beside me in my new life as a widow. Your love is one of God's richest blessings to me.

> To God be all the glory!
> Beth Chilcoat
> Columbus, Ohio
> May 2009

---

[1]See David's speech from the Columbus Young Life 35th Anniversary Banquet, April 9, 2005.

The Chilcoat family

Photograph by Mike Nedell

1 Nathan, 2 Jenny, 3 Toby, 4 Rinnah, 5 Rachel, 6 Beth,
7 Dave, 8 Andy, 9 Michael, 10 Kimie, 11 Kendal, 12 Kayley,
13 Kirsten, 14 Jeff, 15 Katy, 16 Owen, 17 Claire, 18 Abby

Foreword

Though so often hidden from view and avoided by distraction, the truth is that in our world well over a hundred thousand humans die every day. Someone you love, and who loves you, may be ailing and dying. Unthinkable as it is, most of us will lose a parent, spouse, a sibling or a best friend. And, until God ushers in a new order on earth, you and I will also die.

Are we dying well?

God offers us a choice to die to self and live for Him in such a way that neither death nor heaven will seem like such a shock. Likewise in the inevitable reality of suffering, we are given a choice to either run from God, or to run to God. To hide from God, or to hide ourselves in Him.

Dave Chilcoat shows us how to die into the love and hope of eternal life with God and with those who love Him. He shares the raw honesty of pain and sorrow, mixed with humor and hope that only God could give a man so aware of the demise of his mortal flesh. His journal shines light on the realities of illness and death in a fallen world, and also the abundance of God's love and hope of eternity.

This book will help us consider and prepare for life before and after death. It is a gift for any person who would number his days aright and graft his life into the One who defeated death and will live forever. And how rare for a person in such physical pain to make such effort, and find such language – a treasure of hope in the darkness that we all encounter as the world now stands.

Woven into the story of Dave's battle with ALS are golden threads — Scripture, humor and the tenacious love between a man and a woman. We also find a Savior who doesn't just hate death but enters into the fear and darkness and pain of it as Friend and Lover and Life. Who empowers a dying man to think of others. To laugh. To believe. To praise. As with Job, the devil must hate that very much. Through such faith and praise, the Kingdom of God is advanced on the earth.

What an excellent guide Dave is, alongside us in death and life. Wise people everywhere will be blessed by his journey. What he proclaimed to thousands in life, he experienced deeply in death, and continues to share here: that the Gospel is the only hope for life, and death, and life again, forever.

Kelly Monroe Kullberg
Columbus, Ohio
May 2009

Introduction

O n October 28, 2003, David Chilcoat was diagnosed with Amyotrophic Lateral Sclerosis (ALS), known more commonly as Lou
Gehrig's disease. ALS is a disease for which there is no treatment and
no cure. It is 100% fatal, with an average life expectancy of eighteen
months to five years. The first sign of ALS is typically a slight weakness in one area of the body, which progresses until its victim loses all
muscle control, and ultimately the ability to breathe.

My name is Beth Chilcoat and David Chilcoat was my husband.

David and I began our life together on staff for Young Life in
Pittsburgh. Days after the birth of our first child, we moved to Columbus, Ohio, to establish Young Life in the area. David spent ten years
building the ministry, hanging out with teenagers, laughing and crying and sharing the love of God in Jesus Christ. We had four children.
He was a great dad. He told our kids, and everyone he encountered, of
God's faithfulness. He lived energetically, laughed a lot, flew planes,
played golf and loved the Lord. He became a lawyer, practiced law for
25 years and never missed a chance to share the Gospel. He was my
dear husband, my best friend and a child of God. With his diagnosis,
our circumstances changed dramatically, but God did not.

From the outset of the ALS journey, the pain and loss were
devastating. Perhaps hardest was simply to comprehend the fact that
life as we knew it was coming to an end. My vital, 55-year-old husband, so full of energy and passion, was dying. Yet day-by-day, as we
watched ALS literally steal David's health and strength, we watched

the more amazing miracle of God giving David spiritual strength in even greater abundance.

I saw this miracle with my own eyes. And I experienced it myself as God gave me strength to "have a life" in the midst of such pain. David and I came to know God's joy and His enabling power as He walked us though those difficult years.

David faced ALS head-on and was light-years ahead of me in accepting its consequences. I prayed that God would heal. He prayed that God would be glorified. Even the first day, when the family gathered, he set the tone for what was to come, assuring us of God's love, and eventually bringing us to laughter, as only he could. As he battled the disease, David grieved for his family, but celebrated every moment with us, finding comfort in the knowledge that God loved us more than he did and He would surely care for us.

David and I grieved together for our coming loss but chose to live the days we were given to the fullest; to go for it, and see and do everything our remaining time would allow. We traveled a great deal because we knew our time was short, not only because of David's impending death, but also because the degenerative nature of the disease would make it increasingly difficult. We had always been busy people, so the gift of time together made every day bittersweet. We were doing this together, and from that precious perspective we wanted to be sure God got the glory for every moment we shared.

David captured and commented on his experience of life in dying through an online journal. It was a candid account of parallel progression – physical decay and spiritual growth. Like the Psalmist, he described his situation, poured out his heart and witnessed to God's presence in it all.

David wrote weekly for nearly three years and his account was read by tens of thousands around the world. Most entries were divided into three sections: *How am I doing*, *What am I learning*, and *New prayer requests*. For this book, many entries were omitted or compressed. The complete journal is available on the Internet through www.bethchilcoat.com.

The journal became David's legacy and writing it became a passion. In time, even the effort of typing became too costly, and David switched to voice-recognition software. Fortunately his voice remained strong to the end.

Many people suffer without hope. By God's grace, David found joy while suffering. He believed his suffering would not be wasted and that God would use it for His glory. While he lived, he took every opportunity to share God's promise of eternal life in Jesus. I believe he would be pleased that the message continues here.

My prayer is that this book points you toward hope and intimacy with God. Through Scripture, David's words, and your time with the questions and reflections at the end, may you find reason for that hope in your life.

This is the heart of the journal and the journey...

Prologue
Taken from Dave's Personal Diary

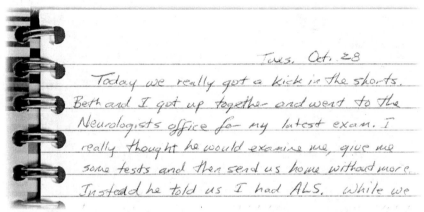

Tues. Oct. 28

Today we really got a kick in the shorts. Beth and I got up together and went to the Neurologists office for my latest exam. I really thought he would examine me, give me some tests and then send us home without more. Instead he told us I had ALS. While we

knew it was a possibility, we really did not think he would tell us that. I have suspected I might have it for a couple of weeks, but Beth was really surprised. The doctor was great, but how do you deal with that news? We got in the car and cried.

On the drive home, we discussed how we would tell the kids. I called Jeff when we got home, and both he and I bawled. We tried Mike and Jenny next; when we couldn't reach them, I drove over to Mom's. Katy, Jeff and Abby were already there. Katy my daughter and I hugged; we all cried together. Dear Mom looked so panicked. I sat her down and told her, and we held each other. I knew she was feeling such pain for her son.

When I got back home, Jeff and Mike came over, then went to the high school to find Andy, but he got home on his own for lunch. Nathan had emailed Jenny at Cedarville College, but she had a full day of make-up classes to teach. The poor thing had to get the news, then wait until after dinner to drive home.

We ended up with all the kids, grandkids and Mom together. We had a great time praying, crying and even laughing together. Friends and extended family showed up. What a difficult day. Still, God has put me in a good place because he has greatly built up my faith over the last ten years or so.

But life changed instantly. So much doesn't matter anymore. The only things that are important are God and other people. I was in constant prayer all day and God met me at every turn.

Beth and I clung to each other. What a woman God gave me those 35 years ago. She is awesome. I hurt so badly for her. She is my pal, my best friend.

My emotions are all over the place. I'm asking God lots of questions but I am surprised that I have not asked why. I do not think that matters. God is on his throne. He loves me and he will care for us and supply all our needs. I want this to bring glory to God. I lift him up. It is not about Beth or me.

Sleep was tough.

Throughout the night, my muscles twitched but God and I talked a lot. He is truly the Comforter. He is my strength. Together we got through the night. Thank God that all our kids and their wonderful spouses know Christ. God is good!

Scriptures that help:

"The LORD is my shepherd, I shall not be in want. He makes me lie down in green pastures, he leads me beside quiet waters, he restores my soul…" (Psalm 23)

"Praise the LORD, O my soul; all my inmost being, praise his holy name. Praise the LORD, O my soul, and forget not all his benefits…" (Psalm 103)

"Don't worry at all then about tomorrow. Tomorrow can take care of itself! One day's trouble is enough for one day." (Matthew 6:34)

"The Christian can even welcome trouble. When all kinds of trials and temptations crowd into your lives my brothers, don't re-sent them as intruders, but welcome them as friends! Realise that they come to test your faith and to produce in you the quality of endurance. But let the process go on until that endurance is fully developed, and you will find you have become men of mature character with the right sort of independence. And if, in the process, any of you does not know how to meet any particular problem he has only to ask God..." (James 1:2-5a)

CHAPTER 1

Winter
We Still Have a Life

December 3, 2003

On the personal front, we know that God loves us and will use this illness for his kingdom. At the same time, we are human and have times of sadness and tears.

After three doctors confirmed my diagnosis, it is hard to say this is just a dream and it will go away. I do not want to be sick. We pray for God's healing every day but are willing to bear this as long as he wants to use it for his purposes.

After visiting doctors at The Ohio State University Hospital, we are sure the only way I can be healed is by God's action alone. They told us that, not only are there no treatments for the disease, but also researchers are not even trying to find a cure since they have no idea what causes ALS. All current research efforts are simply to extend life and hold off the disease as long as possible.

Although there was not much good news, they did tell me I appear to be in the early stages. So Beth and I simply must trust in our most trustworthy Savior, Jesus Christ, and wait on him for all of our needs. We are living one day at a time.

When we face trials and hopelessness, we can have unlimited confidence in a Savior who is limitless in His love.

December 15, 2003

I've had a difficult time physically the last few days.

Sunday, my three sons and I drove to Pittsburgh to the Steelers game. Friends from church gave us tickets and, as life-long Steelers fans, there was no question as to whether we would go even though it was 30° with snow. The Pittsburgh police could not direct us to handicapped parking, so I had to walk a long way. I am not supposed to push myself physically, which is awfully hard for an old jock like me. After walking so far on Sunday, I had real trouble walking at all on Monday and Tuesday. My legs cramped up and were weak.

Sons Andy, Jeff and Mike with Dave

I am trying to go into the office three mornings a week and today was one of those days. Unfortunately, my belly started cramping up so badly, my law partners had to get my muscle relaxants for me and drive me home. I could not even stay for my client appointments.

December 27, 2003

I walk with a funny gait and have lousy balance. When I took the Christmas wreaths down from our windows yesterday and tried to put the screens back up, I fell backwards in slow motion into one of our bushes in the front yard. It was kind of funny, lying there like a turtle on its back, trying to figure out how I was going to get out. I ended up continuing my backwards roll onto the sidewalk. I hope none of our neighbors saw my stunt because they might realize I will not qualify for the Olympics this year. But do not worry. I am still really good looking.

What amazes Beth and me is that, in this lousy, seemingly hopeless situation, we can have a life. Each morning when we pray together, we give God the day and he gives us comfort, peace and love enough for that day. "Don't worry at all then about tomorrow. Tomorrow can take care of itself! One day's trouble is enough for one day." (Matthew 6:34) We are amazed that we are really enjoying our life. God gives us everything we need, just like he promised.

January 6, 2004

Beth and I have traveled to Arizona for me to receive antioxidants administered intravenously. I must admit I was very skeptical about nontraditional medical treatments. However, I am surprised by how good I feel. While there is no question that I remain seriously ill, the trip has been worth it. Beth returned home today. I will stay for another couple weeks to see how much help I can get for the cramping.

What Am I Learning? *One of the main issues I have faced since the doctors told me I am dying is how quickly my emotions surface. There is much sorrow and sadness, not only for me, but for those I love. How do I comfort them and help them through the process? It is very hard.*

Beth and I had a difficult time saying goodbye to each other at the airport. We have not been apart for more than a couple hours since my diagnosis and now we will be apart for two weeks. Our time together has become so precious that we do not want to waste any of it.

God could heal me. However, he may not. I may not have the time I have carelessly come to count on with my loved ones.

I cannot help but have real times of sadness when facing things I loved to do but now find beyond my ability. Beth and I drove to Sedona, Arizona, to see the beautiful rock formations. At one spot we parked the car and walked up the trail to get closer to the mountains. We have had many opportunities over the years to climb mountains and hike trails all over the world. After about 100 yards, we had to turn back because, with the altitude and the rough trail, I could not do it. It made me so sad, I cried. It can be very hard.

When we cannot seem to get by our sadness, we have asked God for encouragement and he has given it to us. A couple nights ago, when I had not had a serious cramp for about five days, I started to think I was actually done with the cramping. Then, without warning, while dining in a restaurant, I got three awful abdominal cramps in a row. Not only did it affect me physically, but emotionally as well. Beth and I held hands and bowed our heads. She simply told God of our pain and asked him to give us a little encouragement. Within a minute, a man walked up and introduced himself. He had seen us praying and he wanted to thank us for not being ashamed of the Gospel. We told him of my ALS. This retired missionary then shared that his new ministry was prayer. He told us he prayed most of each night since he did not sleep well, and he assured us that he would pray faithfully for us. Time and time again, God has answered our prayers for encouragement. Never have we had to wait long.

January 15, 2004

I have been in Arizona for almost three weeks and I feel like a little kid away at summer camp, lonely and homesick. I will meet with the doctor this afternoon to see when I get to go home; it's like waiting on the decision of the parole board. I just pray I'll be home with my family and friends soon.

It's been a rough couple of days. I came down with a bad flu over the weekend. By Monday, I was feeling well enough to go back for treatments, but I did not feel like myself until this morning. I am not sure I have felt that bad at any time in my life. I could not keep anything in me, so I could not keep my medicine down. I ended up with both the flu and my old friend, severe abdominal cramping. It was one weekend I would like to forget.

It feels so strange and lonely to know I am, in a way, different than the rest of the world. I am no longer an average guy. I now have a handicapped badge on my car and I walk funny. I want to go back and be normal again. Yet I know the ultimate answer rests only with God, who loves me and has a plan for this illness and for me.

What Am I Learning? *I wish you could crawl inside my head and see what I am seeing and experiencing. Not because I want you to be sick, but because, when you know you have no earthly hope of getting out alive, you begin to see things from God's perspective.*

Why is it that we are all dying and yet somehow we never really think much about it? Before my diagnosis, I was intellectually aware I was going to die, but there was no immediacy to my situation and, therefore, no urgency to wholeheartedly follow God and his plan for me. Oh, I was a real believer and I worked at my walk with God, but I also did a lot of what I wanted, without checking with God first.

Once a physician looked me in the face and told me I am dying, I became aware that God is not kidding. There is nothing else as important as my relationship with him and my need to be totally his. With no worldly hope, I must finally turn to God without pretense, in total honesty and surrender. What else can I do? Without him I am lost.

I am back in Columbus on a work release program. At least that is what it feels like. The doctor let me come home from Arizona, but after three weeks away, there was so much to do at home I feel like I am working again. Actually, it feels pretty good. It is great to be back with the family.

The trip home was grueling. Because I was a single adult, traveling alone on a one-way ticket, I practically got strip-searched at the airport. Then I had to walk a lot and change planes in Detroit. By the time I got to Columbus, I was exhausted.

I have to admit I am handicapped. I have to get help in airports, and I need a wheelchair between planes. It is hard to admit my life has changed so dramatically.

Being disabled is not all bad, especially when you get to leave ten degree temperatures with snow and ice in Columbus, and go to Disney World with some of your granddaughters. With my funny gait and my larger than life midsection, I think several small children mistook me for one of the Disney characters.

Since I was equipped with an electric wheelchair in the Magic Kingdom, all my grandkids wanted to ride with me. I successfully ignored the warning label, "Carry no passengers." After all, I am an attorney, so I know another attorney wrote that to avoid litigation. One hotel we visited charged $7 for parking, but the handicapped parking was free. See, I told you there are some real advantages to having a disease!

What Am I Learning? *I am not feeling as discouraged. God has given us an understanding that this is our new life. It is interesting to realize I am not feeling the sadness about my inability to walk that I felt just a few weeks ago. Instead, I am feeling that walking slowly with a funny gait is my new reality, so we will just* *live with it. Somehow God is helping us to accept what he has given us, and to know that we will be fine.*

When we were first diagnosed, we desperately brought our specific needs to God. Beth felt we needed to pray for peace, comfort and strength: peace because we felt so desperate and anguished inside, comfort because our hearts truly felt broken, and strength because the future looked so bleak. After about a week she felt led to add joy to the list. We were somewhat confused by the issue of joy. When facing a death sentence it is easy to understand our need for comfort, peace and strength, but joy?

"I am the vine itself, you are the branches...apart from me you can do nothing at all. I have told you this so that you can share my joy, and that your happiness may be complete." (John 15:5, 11)

If Jesus is the vine and we are just branches, what is the responsibility of the branch?

The branch's main job is to sit there and let the vine feed it all the nutrients from the roots so that it will be strong enough to bear fruit. Without God's nutrients flowing through us, we are worthless for anything of eternal value.

Often I have tried to run my life my own way. I have made decisions without consulting God, and have bent things to fit my agenda. The results of my manipulations were not what God had in mind, and I ended up not feeling good about myself.

This illness has caused Beth and me to turn to God each day. We know there is no possible way we can deal with this on our own. As we submit to being the branches, we are experiencing life the way it was designed; we are experiencing God's joy.

There is real freedom in coming face to face with a situation totally beyond our ability and control. No amount of hard work or manipulation can change the circumstances or alter the outcome. It is all in God's hands. He has been good to his word and supplied us with joy. Yes, it can be bittersweet, but it is real joy.

I am holding my own. I played nine holes of golf a couple days ago. A handicapped flag on my cart allowed me to go directly to my ball. I thought it was to warn all the other golfers about my game and to clear the course in front of me, but they said it was to help me (I do wonder what that siren and those lights were every time I hit the ball...).

I only played nine holes because I got tired, but I felt so blessed just to be able to play. I even beat the young guys paired with me. That had to make them feel good about their game; I have a terminal disease and I still beat them. Maybe they should try a different sport.

What Am I Learning? *As Beth and I continue on this journey, we find ourselves in a constant, consistent state of prayer. In the earliest days, our prayers were simple. "God, give us healing, peace and comfort. God, please just get us through the next hour. God, let us know you are right here with us."*

I have never understood which prayers God would answer and for which prayers he would remain silent. I have always known there were times when he might say, "No," and there were times when he might say, "Later."

We have obviously been praying for complete healing. We have heard from hundreds of people who are praying for us from as far away as Malaysia. Our church had a wonderful healing service for us. However, I still have significant symptoms. I have not been healed.

We have been praying for a misdiagnosis. So far four physicians have all said I have ALS. It would appear this prayer request has been answered, "No."

We have also been praying for remission, that the disease would be stopped dead in its tracks. On this I believe God has answered, "Yes," or at least, "Yes for now." My cramps stay at bay, and I feel just as good as when I left Arizona three weeks ago.

We have been praying for wisdom. "And if, in the process, any of you does not know how to meet any particular problem, he has only to ask God – who gives generously to all men without making them feel foolish or guilty – and he may be quite sure that the necessary wisdom will be given him." (James 1:5) We asked for wisdom with regard to treatment. God led us to a doctor in Arizona who has been very helpful.

We have asked God to use this disease and the suffering we are experiencing to lift up Christ for his kingdom. Daily we are seeing the answers to those prayers. God has been putting people in our path who want to know about him and about how we are experiencing his love.

We pray for peace, comfort, strength and joy and we are answered affirmatively. God meets us at every turn and gives us everything we need to face this illness.

The impact of God's faithfulness in our situation has been phenomenal for our whole family. If I had to choose between going back to our previous lives or continuing to have ALS, having learned what we have learned so far, I would choose the disease.

February 15, 2004

We're back home again. This week I had discussions with my disability insurance carrier and with Social Security. I will be declared totally disabled. From a work perspective, that is probably correct. I have to sleep a lot; I have difficulty walking, I have cramping issues that can strike at any time, and I do not have much stamina; all of which make working hard.

From a different perspective, things are not so bad. I have time to spend in the scriptures and to write. I have time to minister in ways I did not have before, and for great conversations with people about Christ. And if I want to talk about Christ, nobody is going to tell a dying guy to shut up.

I have had a tough time the last couple days. I am back in Arizona for treatments, away from Beth and the family. That always makes it harder.

When I sit down to watch television or to read, I feel normal. I begin to think I am getting better. I feel as though I could get up and go for a jog or go to the gym to work out. How can I be sick and feel so good?

Then I get up to walk and I know I am not well.

What Am I Learning? *I hate being sick. I want to feel good again. I want to play golf and work out. I want to go back to my job and work with my clients.*

I want a miracle.

If I look at the situation only from my perspective, this stinks. But life really is not about me. If God is using this illness for good to draw people to Christ, if God is changing and growing my faith through it, if others' faith is being strengthened and changed because of it, if our family is learning to live in total dependence on God's power daily, who am I to argue with God? Perhaps these are the miracles.

As much as I do not like being sick, if that is part of God's plan, why would I want anything different? Perhaps this is God's way of telling me, as he told Paul, that his grace is sufficient. (2 Corinthians 12:9)

CHAPTER 2

Spring
Coming into Deep Waters

March 7, 2004

One really exciting thing they told me at the ALS clinic at Ohio State was that as the disease progresses, I will burn a lot more calories. Therefore, they do not want me to lose any weight or to diet. I always knew there was a silver lining. I get to eat anything I want (although they do say to keep a balanced diet) and eventually I will get down to fighting weight. Eat your hearts out, you dieters. No more Adkins™. No more WeightWatchers®. Just a beautiful, svelte, gorgeous ALS guy.

March 14, 2004

It is hard to believe that just a year ago I was pushing over 800 pounds with my legs and over 300 with my arms. Now I am happy just to be able to walk around the block. The disease may be moving slowly by some estimations, but it seems quick to me.

What Am I Learning? *I have believed that Jesus was God and that he died for me since a starry night in June 1962 at Young Life's Frontier Ranch in Colorado. That night I sat on a rock on the side of Mount Princeton and considered whether or not I* believed in him. I knew he claimed to be the Son of God. People said that if I asked him to live in my heart, I could have my sins forgiven, and God would accept me and give me eternal life with him. I prayed that night and told God what I really thought. "I do not know if you are real or not, but if you are real, I want to be with you. I give my heart to you. So if you are real please let me know." Once I asked him into my heart, there was never again any question he was real, and my life has never been the same.

When I got the bad news about ALS from my doctor, my response was the only one I could make. I have walked with Jesus all these years since 1962. He has always been there for me. I have let him down, but he has never let me down. There have been times when I forgot about him, but he never forgot about me. "I rely on this saying: If we died with him, we shall also live with him; if we suffer with him, we shall also reign with him." (2 Timothy 2:11-12a)

God is always faithful, even when we are not.

Someone asked my youngest son if, in light of all that's happening to me, he would hang in there with his faith. His response was enough to make me cry; he said of course he was going to hang in there. He said there was no way he was going to disrespect his dad.

As awesome as that makes me feel as a father, it also reminds me exactly how I feel about my Heavenly Father. After all these years of his taking care of me, there is no way I could disrespect him now, when the going gets a little rough.

Do not get me wrong. There are certainly hard moments when I feel discouraged. Sometimes Beth and I are overwhelmed by the magnitude of what we are facing.

There is nothing great or noble about my attitude toward my illness. True happiness comes from knowing who I am, and I am a child of God.

Beth and I just finished a weeklong Caribbean cruise. The doctors should really be proud of me now. I successfully ate my way across a few thousand miles of sea, daily consuming a hundred thousand calories of all-you-can-eat shipboard cuisine. Since the ship's showers are very small, by the end of the week I just had them hose me down on deck.

A new problem has cropped up over the last few weeks. My feet and legs are swelling significantly. The doctors say it has nothing to do with my heart. We do not know the cause, but it was worse after riding in the car for two days to get to Florida. I believe it has something to do with my lack of exercise, since the swelling got much better on the days I walked the deck. The cane really helped on the ship and may become a permanent fixture.

Phil Mickelson won a major at last. Since I have ALS and was not able to play this year, I am glad Phil finally won the Masters. I suppose I can no longer become the world-class golfer I always dreamed I could be; except for the ALS, I think I could have even given Tiger a run for that #1 spot. I guess we will never really know unless God heals me, so let's all pray for total healing. And if God heals me, I will be happy to share my winnings with all of you. Maybe a chance at big bucks will be a motivator for you to keep praying.

I am doing well, with no real changes from week to week. Beth and I tried a bike ride on Saturday. I put the bike seat down a few inches so I could balance easier and peddle, using my whole leg without having to extend my toes. Getting on the bike was hard, but once I got rolling, it worked. Because my left side is so weak, I just peddled with my right leg. It was great to get outside and do something fun. We only went about a mile and a half around the neighborhood, but I was on a bike and moving. When I got off, my legs shook from tired muscles. It is strange that after a short ride on level ground, my legs felt like I had run a marathon. Who's complaining though? I still got to ride my bike.

Beth and Dave enjoying the outdoors

April 20, 2004

What Am I Learning? *Beth and I joined our kids and their kids for a weekend in Michigan. We hung out together, laughed and played games, and had a great time together as a family.*

It was late when we arrived back home; Beth mowed the lawn while I tried to unload the car. As I struggled up the two steps to our front entrance, cane in one hand and suitcase in the other, I had a conversation with God about how crummy this disease is. It stinks to have a tough time doing something as easy as unloading the car or getting up a couple steps.

All my life I have been very self-sufficient. Physically, I've been athletic and strong. There was little I was afraid to tackle, and I took great joy and pride in being able to do many things for my family and myself. I was even one of those guys who got up after dinner to clear the table and wash the dishes. (Beth was a good instructor early in our marriage.)

But this weekend was so different. My kids carried bags for me. My grandkids ran errands. My wife mowed the lawn. (She would tell you that she has always mowed the lawn, but at least this time I wanted to mow it.) I sat in a chair and watched them do all the work.

Some of you are probably saying, "What are you complaining about? Sit back and enjoy it."

There is a significant difference between taking a break from work because you want to and taking a break because you can do nothing else. In recent months, I have thought about what I would do if someone tried to mug me or tried to hurt someone in my family. What would I do if I got in a fight? In the past, I thought of myself as able to defend myself or rescue another. Now, I know I would just get hurt. I could not even run away. My forty-yard dash time could be measured using a sundial.

This last week, and periodically since my diagnosis, Beth and I have felt we are getting the tar beaten out of us in a big battle. ALS is fatal and, absent a miracle from God, I will die from it. But this battle is not about ALS or about the way we expected our lives to unfold. Satan would like us to focus on this disease and what I am losing daily. He would like fear to take over our lives. He would like discouragement to reign. He would like depression to steal the joy from our household.

But in Christ, we have the victory! If we resist Satan, he will flee from us. (James 4:7) God promises there will be no temptation greater than we will be able to bear. (1 Corinthians 10:13) We know this is true, because God's Word is true. In this battle of unseen powers of good and evil, God wins.

April 28, 2004

My left leg is getting weaker. I am walking slowly and my feet slap against the ground like I am wearing giant clown shoes.

May 5, 2004

I just spent a couple days away with friends whom I have known and loved for forty years. What an awesome time we had together as we shared the scriptures and prayed. It was a privilege to share time with men who have truly committed their lives to Jesus. If only the world could know the depth of friendship available in Christ.

I played golf while away and still had fun. I was afraid to warm up because I only have so many swings in these weak legs. After a 47 on the front side, I started to get it together and finished with a 41 on the back. It was not my best, but who cares? I played the backside well and I was playing. God is good.

What Am I Learning? *"You are dying and there is nothing we can do about it."*

Those devastating words were the beginning of a new life for Beth and me. As we sat in the examination room at the neurologist's office, we just stared at the doctor. "Over time, you will lose the use of the muscles in your arms and legs. You will be a quadriplegic. Eventually it will affect your speech and your ability to swallow. Finally, it will affect your diaphragm and you will die of respiratory failure." It was incredibly ugly news.

All my life I have suffered from asthma. As a wrestler I had to start getting in shape months before the other guys because my lungs did not work as well. Not being able to breathe has always been terribly frightening to me. I can remember, as a kid during an asthma attack, just concentrating on the next breath. Now the doctor was telling me I am going to suffocate to death. It scares me so badly I do not even know how to describe it.

How can I go on? Every time I think about the future, I get scared.

How can Beth and I keep from ruining the days we do have with constant worry about what could or would happen? How can we keep the fear of future loss from paralyzing us in the present, taking away any joy and peace we may have?

In that first desperate day, I read Matthew 6:34: "Don't worry at all then about tomorrow. Tomorrow can take care of itself! One day's trouble is enough for one day." Such a comforting verse.

Maybe I do not have to worry about the future, about what tomorrow will bring. Maybe my job is simply to live one day at a time.

But how do we stop worry from creeping in? How do we plan? There are times in our lives when we must plan. By involving God in our decisions we can plan according to his will.

When we found out I am ill, Beth and I knew that we did not have the facilities in our home to deal with the handicaps I might face. Through prayer, we determined we should build an addition to our house, a sunroom that we will enjoy if God heals me or I am in remission. On the other hand, if the illness continues its course, we can easily use it as a bedroom. We are simply waiting on God to tell us if we built a sunroom or a bedroom.

I now begin each day by giving it to God as his day. It is the only day I have; I cannot know what the future holds. But today, God has given me a gift: to live one more day as his child. What an awesome gift for me to enjoy and, as I give it back to him, what joy it produces as I see how he uses it.

How can we not trust the God who loves us perfectly and who has wondrous plans for us beyond what we could hope or imagine? "For I know the plans I have for you," declares the Lord, "plans to prosper you and not to harm you, plans to give you hope and a future." (Jeremiah 29:11)

May 12, 2004

As good as last week was, this week was not. I felt weak and exhausted. There were more spasms in my right leg than in the past. I need that leg to drive.

What Am I Learning? *"Save me, O God, for the waters have come up to my neck. I sink in the miry depths, where there is no foothold. I have come into the deep waters; the floods engulf me. I am worn out calling for help; my throat is parched." (Psalm 69:1-3a)*

I woke up Monday and my legs felt like lead. When I stood up, there was no strength in them. It was like trying to stand on wet spaghetti. I tried to play golf with friends from church, but I could not make my legs work. By the seventh hole, I gave up. At the turn I got in the car and went home. I cried most of the way. I was in deep water. There was no foothold. When I got home, nothing got better. Beth and I prayed for healing, but my throat was parched.

Tuesday, I woke exhausted. I went to my men's Bible study, prayed and came home. I was depressed. I went to bed at 1:30 in the afternoon and slept until 5:00. I awoke feeling no better. That evening I walked home from my daughter Jenny's house. The two or three blocks took about 30 minutes. I was walking in five feet of water. I awoke this morning with a cloud over me.

Oh Lord, I know you are real. I know you love me and that I am yours. But Lord, I feel like I am lost. It is so dark. I am so down. There is so much I have lost. There is so much I can no longer do. I've always been the "go-to guy" in the family, and now I cannot even tie my shoes. What do I do, Lord? How do I crawl out of this pit? My emotions are right under the surface. I cry out for your help, Lord.

As I left my office today, hobbling to the car with my cane and my briefcase, I encountered an acquaintance whose office is in the same building. He saw my cane and asked if I had hurt myself. When I told him I have Lou Gehrig's disease, he told me to take it easy and have a good day. He had no idea how to react to such terrible news. The water is rising.

I still mourn for the things I have lost. I watch the tears in my children's eyes when I am not doing well. I know my wife is hurting when she curls up on the couch beside me and just hugs me. The water is up to my neck. There is nothing I can do to make them feel better.

"But I pray to you, O Lord, in the time of your favor; in your great love, O God, answer me with your sure salvation. Rescue me from the mire, do not let me sink; deliver me from those who hate

me, from the deep waters. Do not let the floodwaters engulf me or the depths swallow me up or the pit close its mouth over me. Answer me, O Lord, out of the goodness of your love; in your great mercy turn to me. Do not hide your face from your servant; answer me quickly, for I am in trouble. Come near and rescue me; redeem me because of my foes." (Psalm 69:13-18)

When I got home today, there were eight men working on our new addition. They were doing work I like to do. I have always loved building and carpentry. If I was healthy, there are few things I would rather do to relax than work with my hands, but I cannot do anything like that now. I have a basement full of tools and equipment that just sit.

I need to pray, Lord.

"Even though I walk through the valley of the shadow of death, I will fear no evil, for you are with me; your rod and your staff, they comfort me." (Psalm 23:4)

God, give me what I need right now to get by and to keep my eyes focused on you. Lord, I will praise your name, because you are the only thing I can hold onto in this high water. You are my God, the rock of my salvation. I will cling to you as the waters swirl around me.

CHAPTER 3

Summer
Reaching for the Higher Things

June 10, 2004

Our son Andy has graduated, and the new addition is finished. There are some minor punch list items to be completed on both, but the addition is clean, has furniture and looks great. Andy's room is definitely not clean, but he does have some furniture for college and he certainly looks great. On final inspection today, the addition passed. The high school gave Andy a diploma, so we guess he passed, too. Life should slow down a bit now.

I went to the ALS clinic yesterday, and I am doing pretty well. There is some progression of the disease, but it is moving very slowly. My left leg is slightly worse than last time. The color change in that leg is due to muscle loss, which causes the tissue to retain more blood. The result is the left leg is significantly redder than the right, and I have a two-tone look when I am wearing shorts. Just think, you have to pay extra for a two-tone paint job when you buy a car!

As Beth and I left the clinic, I commented on how strange it was to be parked in handicapped parking. In my head I am the same guy as before, but my body just does not know it.

Dave and Beth flank new graduate Andy

June 17, 2004

Monday was our 35th wedding anniversary, and I want to share with you the most wonderful greeting card[2] my wife ever bought for me. It says, "Your heart, so humble and loving, is the vessel God uses to pour his goodness into my life, our home and our marriage. Through the years, the vessel has been reshaped and weathered through challenges and joys that are ever-changing, but your heart has always been willing to be pliable in the Master's hands – and that is what makes you a man after God's heart...and the man who has won mine. For all that you are and all that you are becoming, you have my respect, my admiration and my love – completely. Happy Anniversary."

Even typing it out makes me cry.

[2] Copyright® DaySpring Cards. Used by Permission.

The fasciculations (little spasms in my muscles) seem stronger to me. I get about sixty a minute. They are not much of a bother except when they are intense in my bigger muscles or deep in my abdomen. At those times they are uncomfortable.

Lately my hands are giving me some trouble. I first noticed it when I had trouble pushing the door button to open my car. I also have had trouble clipping my fingernails. My hands concern me because I want to be able to type on my computer, as well as continue to care for myself. But it is not bad yet.

What Am I Learning? *"Praise the Lord, O my soul; all my inmost being, praise his holy name." (Psalm 103:1)*

Oh Lord, how do I praise you? All my life I have petitioned you for my needs and my wants. I have sought you when I am in pain and suffering. I have pleaded with you for my desires. For most of my life it has been about me. So now, how do I praise you?

"Praise the Lord, O my soul, and forget not all his benefits." (Psalm 103:2)

Everything I have that is worthwhile is a gift from you. My wife, my kids, my grandkids are all from your mercy and grace. My joy, my strength, my comfort, my peace are all from you. How can I not praise you every living moment of the day? You are my strength and my shield, my hope in all my troubles.

"...Who forgives all your sins and heals all your diseases, who redeems your life from the pit..." (Psalm 103:3-4a)

Oh Lord, how is it possible for me not to praise your name when you have sent your Son to die for me so my sins are forgiven? How is it possible for me to not praise your name when you have cleansed me of all unrighteousness so I can live with you forever. I still carry the scars of my sins, but Lord, those scars show your glory because they shout out that you truly have loved me and healed me. I will praise you because I know you are trustworthy and loving. Your Son has given his life for me, this lost and wounded child. Praise you, Father.

"...*And crowns you with love and compassion, who satisfies your desires with good things so that your youth is renewed like the eagle's.*" *(Psalm 103:4b-5)*

Lord, what joy it is to wake up in the morning to your presence, to know you are there. You care for me in even the smallest ways. You know the number of hairs on my head. You satisfy me with good things. Oh Lord, how you fill me up so I feel like I could fly. In my lowest of times you bear me up on eagle's wings. I feel like a child who faces the day without a care in the world because he is loved and his father is watching over him. How can I be afraid? You are there.

"*As for man, his days are like grass, he flourishes like a flower of the field; the wind blows over it and it is gone, and its place remembers it no more.*" *(Psalm 103:15-16)*

Someday, like the grass, I will be gone and the earth will no longer even remember I was here. This life is but a fleeting moment in eternity. But because of you, Oh Lord, I will live forever.

Since things have slowed down, I am looking forward to having quiet time with Beth. Now that I think about it, after thirty-five years of putting up with me, maybe she needs some time away from me...too bad. She is stuck with this overweight ALS guy who will not let her go.

I am doing surprisingly well. My hands are holding their own, and the cramping is still at bay. Since my feet and toes do not work well, it is hard to balance. I fell down the stairs at a golf club the other day. I did not get hurt, but it was embarrassing. I made a rather grand entrance as I tripped on the stairs, rolled forward and crashed through the swinging doors into the men's locker room. In the old days, I would have jumped right up, yelled, "Tah Dah!" and taken a bow. Now it takes longer to drag myself up on my cane. The old soft shoe is not what it used to be. I may be the only guy who needs to play golf with kneepads, elbow pads and a crash helmet.

What Am I Learning? *In my situation, death is a constant in the equation. With that in mind, the thing most changed in my relationship with Christ is my confidence in his victory over death.*

"So when the perishable is lost in the imperishable, the mortal lost in the immortal, this saying will come true: Death is swallowed up in victory. For where now, O death, is your power to hurt us? Where now, O grave, is the victory you hoped to win?" (1 Corinthians 15:54-55)

God promised me that, since I have put my faith and trust in his Son, Jesus, I will live with him for eternity. I am so confident in this that I am staking my life on it.

July 20, 2004

Beth and I were on our thirty-fifth anniversary trip to Europe these last two weeks, thanks to her mom and brother. The European definition of "handicapped accessible" must be a little different from ours. Of course there is that small problem of making thousand-year-old streets – most of them cobblestone or gravel – handicapped accessible. We had so much trouble with the wheelchair that we actually bent one of the wheels. There were many steps without elevators or ramps where I just had to get out and work my way up the stairs. Plus, since I find myself sweating through my clothes if I walk very far, I'm truly an attractive guy when I hobble up to people, smelling like I just spent the last hour in the gym.

Meanwhile I'm having trouble buttoning my pants. Maybe I'll just get a bunch of sweatpants with elastic tops. I could even sell them at my new chain of stores, "ALS R US."

Today the doctors told us ALS does not affect sexual performance, for which I am very happy.

What Am I Learning? *I talked to a man yesterday who has had ALS for years. That is supposed to make me happy, because he has long out-lived his life expectancy. However, all it did was depress me.*

It is terribly difficult to think about living as a captive in my own body. He cannot walk or use his hands. He is confined to a wheelchair and can only get out when someone helps him. He cannot feed himself or go to the bathroom without help.

Death is a daunting challenge, but living for years without my body seems even more so.

My balance is worse. Falling down is not so bad, but when I fell in the garage and threw my favorite coffee cup onto the concrete, I got upset. You can do a lot to a guy and get away with it, but do not mess with his favorite coffee mug. It was one of those stainless steel ones and it is now flat on one side. When I replace it, I may look for one machined out of heavy gauge steel. I may not be able to keep from falling, but I know I will continue to drink coffee.

What Am I Learning? *A friend of mine died a few days ago. Doug's death capped off a really lousy week. How do I find God's peace?*

"Here is a last piece of advice. If you believe in goodness and if you value the approval of God, fix your minds on the things which are holy and right and pure and beautiful and good." (Philippians 4:8)

God, I challenge you. I will try to focus on the good things and see if they outnumber the bad things:

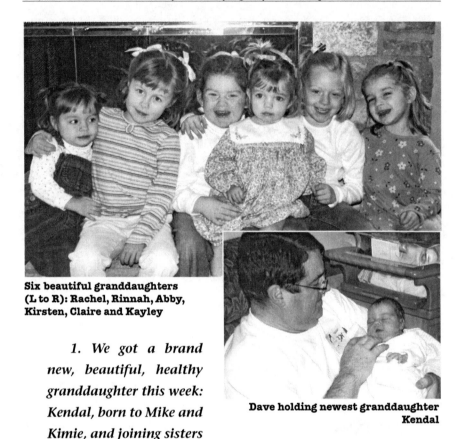

Six beautiful granddaughters
(L to R): Rachel, Rinnah, Abby,
Kirsten, Claire and Kayley

Dave holding newest granddaughter
Kendal

1. We got a brand new, beautiful, healthy granddaughter this week: Kendal, born to Mike and Kimie, and joining sisters Kayley and Kirsten. That is pretty hard to beat, but she is a girl again. In fact, number seven out of seven. How long will we have to endure all these little girls, God? Just kidding.

Okay, one point for God.

2. Jenny is pregnant with grandchild number eight. The ultrasound showed that this baby has a "thingy;" a grandson at last. What else could a "thingy" be?

Another point for God.

3. We are also looking forward to Katy giving birth to grandbaby number nine. Oh, all right, the Chilcoats are good at grandchildren (and you know I've always been competitive).

Thanks, God. One point.

4. Mike invited his brother Andy to help run the program

40

at Young Life's Rockbridge camp in Virginia. It was awesome to watch my sons entertaining the kids. And Andy will be living with a bunch of Christian guys at Ohio State this fall. That is obviously better than living in a crack house or spending the fall in jail.

I will give that one to you, too, God.

So far there are more good things than bad on my ledger.

5. Every morning when I wake up, my dog Lou will not leave me alone until he gets up on my chest and licks my face.

He really likes me, but I am only giving you half a point, God, because the licking part is not so great.

6. I do have an awesome wife, God. Thanks for loaning her to me for these 35 years. She drives me crazy with the honey-do list, but she is awesome. She is my best friend and she is really hot!

Okay, I will give you two points for her.

7. My new room is really great. I am sitting here with all the windows open. The fan is going. It feels like I am outside. What a nice place to be when I cannot get out.

One more point for you.

8. Our kids married great spouses. All the little cousins like each other and there is so much happy noise. Well, it is awfully noisy but how else could it be? Could we get grand-kids with volume controls attached? I doubt it.

God definitely gets one point here.

9. I get all the sports channels on my new big plasma television. The TV is great, God, but the problem is that the Pittsburgh Pirates still really stink.

I will give you a point for the TV but you owe me a half point for the lousy Pirates. I have been a loyal fan for 48 years, but a lot of good that has done me.

10. God, you and I are great friends. We spend time together every day, and whenever I call on you, even in the

night, you are there. You never let me down. You are always faithful, even when I am faithless.

I have to give you at least ten points for this one.

"To you, who were spiritually dead all the time that you drifted along on the stream of this world's ideas of living, and obeying its unseen ruler...to you Christ has given life." (Ephesians 2:1-2)

If I want to feel sorry for myself, how is this fair, God? How many points do you get for eternal life? There is no way to count. You are wrecking the competition.

But I still have one arrow left in my quiver. I have ALS. I know I am supposed to be concentrating on the good and this might be hitting below the belt, but it is hard to feel your peace when I am so sick.

Yet how can I whine when you have given me so many blessings in this life, as well as life with you for eternity?

With a thankful heart, overflowing with the knowledge of your many blessings, I will reach out for the higher things of heaven as I live for you now.

CHAPTER 4

Fall
Lessons from the First Year

September 8, 2004

I played a little golf when we were in Wisconsin this week. On one hole I hit the ball, lost my balance, fell down and went into some cramping. I adopted a hand wave to the other guys when I went down, like a water skier, so that they would know I was okay. Golf truly has become a contact sport.

September 18, 2004

Home again. Tobias Nathan Shaw decided to quit torturing our daughter Jenny and get himself born. We finally have one with outside plumbing. Toby is a real joy.

At the ALS clinic this week, we got encouraging news that the disease is progressing slowly. My primary physician confirmed my left side was getting weaker and he observed muscle loss in my legs and in my left hand. But he was optimistic that it may continue to progress slowly. He indicated I might be one of those fortunate ones who live longer than the averages would indicate.

Beth and I made a decision to order a power wheelchair. When we tried to walk a simple trail this weekend, I felt I would fall at any moment. While it is discouraging to get a power wheelchair, I want to be able to stay as active as I can. With a power chair, I can continue to chase Beth into the woods. Perhaps I need to get an all-terrain wheelchair with high-speed gearing.

What Am I Learning? *Night before last in Wisconsin, lying on my back I could not get my breath. I had awakened from a sound sleep as if I was drowning, with no air in my lungs. What was going on? Was my body forgetting to breathe while I was sleeping? If I concentrated on taking a full breath, I could almost get enough air in, but not quite. After a couple minutes, I had to sit up. I did not want to wake Beth because she needed her sleep. Neither of us had slept much the night before. I sat in the dark concentrating on breathing and praying. Periodically throughout the night I fell back asleep, only to wake again without enough air.*

This is really scary, God. Is this the beginning of the respiratory failure the doctors say will ultimately kill me? It seems so early in the disease for that. The doctors said I would probably live three to five years, but so far it has only been eleven months. You know how afraid I am of not being able to breathe, after all those years with asthma when I had to concentrate on nothing but my next breath. Couldn't I have some other kind of disease that would not scare me like this?

Last night I felt much better. At the clinic, the respiratory specialist was sure my problems in Wisconsin were simply related to allergies. But I kept thinking about that fear. I remember back in the early seventies, when I had pneumonia, I felt like I could only breathe with the top inch of my lungs. Fear can be absolutely debilitating.

Today at my granddaughter's soccer game, I held little Kendal Chilcoat, age five weeks. Kendal slept peacefully in my arms, not worrying that I might drop her.

Since I am God's child, there is no reason for me to be afraid either. When I awake and I cannot breathe, fear takes over because breathing is life or death. But God is my father. As his son, I have come to know that he is very, very fond of me. Even if he does not deliver me from the impending disaster, I need to rest in him; he will provide everything I need.

"You will not have to fight this battle. Take up your positions; stand firm and see the deliverance the Lord will give you, O Judah and Jerusalem. Do not be afraid; do not be discouraged. Go out to face them tomorrow, and the Lord will be with you." (2 Chronicles 20:17)

September 28, 2004

If you see a red blur going by on your sidewalk, get out of the way. It may be me. My crazy brother Ed fixed up an old Honda three-wheeled scooter for me so Beth and I can still go riding. It has two wheels in the back and I can step through the frame. Plus it has hand controls. We are putting handicapped signs all over it and calling it a handicapped scooter in the hope that some overzealous park ranger will not give me a ticket for driving a power vehicle on the bike trails. It will actually do about 30 miles per hour, so if they try to ticket me, maybe I can make a run for it. I always liked those movies with the high-speed chase; just call me "Bullet."

I had trouble with my balance when I tried to play golf this week. On one short, twenty-foot chip, I addressed the ball at least ten times and finally just hit it as I was falling. It is hard to admit that I am about at the end of playing. Maybe God will give me the strength to play some more, but I am really mourning the loss of one of my favorite pastimes and passions.

When I get to heaven, I am looking forward to a new body that will allow me to swing in balance. I will arrange a tee time for all of us.

(L to R) Greg Ball, Jeff Chilcoat, Dave, Charlie Knoop and Rob Crocker

October 7, 2004

The Lord has given us gorgeous October weather. Beth and I had fun getting out on our bikes, she on her Trek and me on my red blur motor scooter. We experienced the joy of the wind in our faces and the beautiful outdoors. There have been no park ranger tickets so far, but I've always liked skirting close to the edge of the law. If I were not a follower of Christ, I would have made a great criminal.

I continue to do rather well physically. Today, instead of playing golf, I just rode along with four friends and watched them play. I had a wonderful time with them and a great time being out in the sunshine with my Lord. What better place to pray than in the beauty of a golf course?

I am still able to tickle my grandkids. They just have to come to me to get tortured since I cannot catch them anymore on my own. They must like me, because they put up with it.

I thought I was near the end of my golf career. Well, God has a great sense of humor. This week I played in a charity golf tournament for an organization called Fore Hope, a group that uses golf as a thera- peutic medium for people with disabilities. It was an alternate shot affair pairing a disabled golfer with an able-bodied golfer. The tees for disabled golfers were very short so I never had a shot much over 135 yards. We ended up winning by 7 strokes. There really might be a fu- ture for me on the all-ALS Professional Golfers Tour.

I am experiencing increased cramping in my forearms and hands. While I can live with it, it certainly is painful at times.

Beth and I have been taking our "new" used handicapped van for a test drive – through eight states and about 3,000 miles. Every- thing appears to be working. We brought our Schnauzer Lou with us, but he cannot see out of the windows. Frankly, he could have had the same experience if I had put him in the dryer at home and just bounced him around for a week or two.

Let me tell you the really bad news. Stuck in our hotel room each night, Beth has had to endure endless playoff baseball games with nowhere to get away. But she is a good woman, never even ask- ing to hold the remote.

What Am I Learning? *"As the deer pants for streams of water, so my soul pants for you, O God. My soul thirsts for God, for the living God. When can I go and meet with God? My tears have been my food day and night, while men say to me all day long, 'Where is your God?'" (Psalm 42:1-3)*

Beth and I were on a shuttle bus in Zion National Park and a small herd of mule deer was running to the water of a nearby stream.

Like a deer pants for water, my soul pants for you, O God.

My emotions cry out of me. I mourn for the past, for what I used to have. Yet the past is gone. I am no longer that young kid, running mile after mile, up the mountain at Young Life's Frontier Ranch. I now must rest after I put on my pants. My only hope lies in you, Lord.

Over the last week and a half we have visited Zion, Bryce, Canyonland, Mesa Verde, Arches, Canyon Reef and the North Rim of the Grand Canyon. We drove through the Rockies, visited the Collegiate Range and drove down the Grand Staircase of the Escalonte. We saw some of the most incredible scenery in the world; every park was breathtakingly unique.

As we looked at the grandeur, we were struck by God's amazing creativity. The rabbits here have bigger ears so that they can dissipate the heat of the desert. There are plants we had never seen, designed by God to live in an area without water. How can I look at this incredible creation and not believe there is a God, and that he can handle my future?

Beth and I drove up to Young Life's Frontier Ranch near Buena Vista, Colorado, on the side of Mount Princeton. I stood in the infield, looking above the buildings to the rock where I had sat in 1962, arguing with God. It was there I asked God into my heart. What a change that commitment has made in my life! I do not know what life would have been like without Christ, but I know it would have been lonelier, darker and less joyful. The joy, the peace and the excitement have made it all worthwhile. What a ride it has been.

November 5, 2004

Beth and I arrived safely home from our grand automotive tour of the western world. We covered 5,400 miles in eighteen days and had a great time, but there is no future for me as a long-haul trucker.

I need to hold on to things to get around now. It reminds me of my early days, before I learned to walk, pulling up on the coffee table and holding tight. The only difference is I am not nearly as cute.

Happy travelers on their western adventure

My left thumb gets progressively worse. Today I could not button the buttons on my right shirtsleeve. In the future, I can wear short-sleeved shirts and roll them up. Maybe I should roll up a pack of Lucky Strikes® in my sleeve and be cool.

What Am I Learning? *There is a small glass globe, sitting on my desk, filled with 96 red pencils. Each is about an inch long and no longer able to be sharpened. When I was in law school, Beth and I already had three children and I could not afford highlighters, so I simply bought red pencils to underline my textbooks. As each pencil got too short to sharpen, I threw it in the bottom drawer of my desk. After I graduated and took the bar exam, I remember looking at the pencil stubs and reflecting on all I had learned over the preceding years.*

It is a great exercise to stop and reflect on what we are learning.

October 28th marked the one-year anniversary of my diagnosis with ALS. Such a date is a perfect time to reflect. So much has taken place in our lives since last year. I will limit myself to key lessons that God has seared into our hearts and minds:

Humble yourself before God.

I used to think I was a pretty special guy. I gave credit to God for all my special talents, but if I was honest, I often took a great deal of pride in them. I was proud of what I was able to do for his Kingdom.

It is easy to feel good about myself when I give to the poor or do free legal work for someone in need. But how do I feel good about myself when I am the poor person and I cannot physically do any work? How do I feel when others have to do my work for me?

It was great to be an attorney; I was proud of my ability to advise others. Now I am on disability and retired. I always considered it my responsibility to earn the money my family requires and to take care of all their physical needs. Now I do not earn a paycheck and my wife has to mow the lawn and carry the bags.

"God is always against the proud, but he is always ready to give grace to the humble. So, humble yourselves under God's strong hand, and in his own good time he will lift you up. You can throw the whole weight of your anxieties upon him, for you are his personal concern." (1 Peter 5:5b-7)

How great it is, even as my health fails, to be loved and cared for by the God of the Universe!

Real life comes when we surrender to God.

I am a pilot. My father was a military pilot and, in our family, flying was something that came naturally. I used to tell the Young Life kids that an airplane can be used for things other than flying. For example, you can taxi a plane at speeds up to 60 miles per hour. If your car broke down, you could probably taxi it to the grocery store. However, you would have to really be careful about the propeller in the crosswalks, and the wings would be hard to maneuver around cars and other objects. While it would work, this would not be its best use. An airplane is designed to do something a car cannot do. When the pilot pulls back on the yoke and the wheels leave the ground, the plane does what it was designed for; it is far superior to a car. God designed man to live in relationship with him. While it is possible to live without God, the real adventure comes when we live as we were designed to live. We get to fly with God. What a waste of an airplane to never leave the ground. What a waste of a human being to never experience life as God designed it.

Real life is not about having no pain.

When people ask Christ into their lives, Christians tell them of the joy and happiness they will experience. Rarely, however, do we spend much time talking about suffering and pain. As a dad, I do not want any of my children to suffer. God is my father. Why would he want me to suffer? I know God hurts with me over this disease because he is my dad. He will use this suffering for me to get to know him even better. In that knowledge I will discover real life, eternal life, and I will be complete.

"The man who patiently endures the temptations and trials that come to him is the truly happy man. For once his testing is complete he will receive the crown of life which the Lord has promised to all who love him." (James 1:12)

We are powerless to hold on to what we love.

There are so many things in life we try to hold on to. Some are bad and some are good. I truly love my wife. I truly love and care for all my kids, their spouses and our grandkids. But try as I might, I have discovered I have absolutely no power to hold on to them. While I was always careful to keep my children out of traffic and to make sure that they had all the proper vaccinations, their ultimate protection did not rest with me, but with God. If I am so fortunate that I get to the end of my life and they are all still here and healthy, I still cannot hold onto them. But I can give all those people back to God, who actually has the power to protect them. They will stay here and I will go hang out with Jesus.

This Sunday on the way up the center aisle after church, my legs thought it would be entertaining to do a face plant right in front of a bunch of my friends. Everyone rushed to help me. It is embarrassing to be the center of attention for something as silly as falling down. I am thinking about handing out scoring numbers so, the next time it happens, the crowd can score my dive. If I work at it, I should be able to get all 10s.

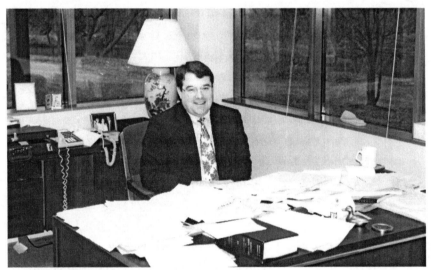

Dave at the law office, his second home

What Am I Learning? *Yesterday I went to my office for the first time in four weeks. As I walked in, I noticed my partners had carried through on their plan to redecorate. It looked good, with new wallpaper and some newly recovered furniture. Out of habit, I walked toward the back and turned left into my office, but there was new furniture and everything was different. Then it struck me. It is no longer my office. It now belongs to one of my partners. When I retired I told my partners they should move someone into my office, because it is one of the bigger ones. I had just forgotten; old habits die hard.*

All of this started me thinking about houses and homes. My office was very comfortable. I spent 50 or 60 hours a week in it for years. In addition to the wonderful home that Beth and I share, this office was a home away from home.

The Bible mentions houses and homes on a number of occasions. "We know, for instance, that if our earthly dwelling were taken down, like a tent, we have a permanent house in Heaven, made, not by man, but by God." (2 Corinthians 5:1)

For me, this temporary dwelling, this tent, is getting weak and rotten. Apart from God healing me, I see that my life will end. This is the hardest thing I have ever had to deal with. I want so much to be with my family and friends and to enjoy all life can offer. I want to see Andy graduate from college and get married. I want to go to all of my grandkids' games and see their school plays. I want to watch them grow up and I want to be the old white-haired guy tickling his eighty-year old wife.

Instead, I must choose to focus on God's promises and to trust that he has my best interest at heart. What comfort to know that, when my tent gives out, I will move into God's house and make it my home.

November 21, 2004

It has been a great weekend. The Buckeyes beat Michigan and my Steelers won their eighth straight.

Last weekend at church, I had the privilege of baptizing my grandson, Toby Shaw. After the baptism, I left church through a side door. It was emotional, baptizing a grandchild, and my voice cracked several times. I later heard several people were concerned about my being so overcome with emotion that I could not come back to the service. The truth was I had tickets for the Browns v. Steelers game in Cleveland and did not want to miss either event. I walked out the side door right into a friend's car. He drove so fast that we cut over a half hour off the trip. What a great Sunday. Baptize Toby and watch the Steelers beat the Browns. Life is really good.

Toby gets to know his Papa

I am doing extremely well. Since coming back from treatments in Arizona, I have continued to get one IV treatment each week at home, which seems to be having the desired effect.

My left hand is weaker and I have a lot of trouble with snaps and buttons. I used to think it was really exciting when Beth helped me get undressed. Now I think it is really exciting when she helps me get dressed. (I am allowed to say that; we are married!)

I am still able to get up and down the stairs, but I only do it once a day. We are hoping I can continue to go upstairs to bed for a long time.

November 29, 2004

This week I saw snow on the deck for the first time this year. Snow used to send me into mourning because it meant golf was over for the season. I always started counting down 120 days from the first snow to the theoretical date for the next golf season.

Since my situation has changed so much, God has given me a new perspective. I believe he wants me to enjoy each new day as it comes, not live in the future. How fun it will be this year to watch the snow fly, to sit in front of the fireplace and to see how God will use each day for his glory. I am so looking forward to the Christmas season and all the little grandkids. This retirement stuff is good.

I just wish I had understood how to live this way before I got sick.

On the emotional side, it is very hard to deal with the fact that I am slowly losing my ability to function on my own. I can still drive because I still have a decent right leg, but there will probably come a day when I have to give it up. The other day, Beth and I had dinner out with friends and I had a difficult time using my fork. I do not think anyone noticed, but I spent a lot of time crying about it that night when Jesus and I were talking. I do not look forward to having someone feed me.

Still, I have learned Jesus does not have a difficult time with my crying on his shoulder about my losses. He understands. And I always come away stronger for it. This is not an easy process, but God is teaching me every day.

CHAPTER 5

Winter
It Is Well with My Soul

December 7, 2004

As soon as I finish writing this, our six granddaughters who are old enough are coming over to work on Christmas presents for their parents. Last year when we did this, it was an absolute zoo, with stickers and glue everywhere. One year we had them weave potholders. It was a great idea at first. Then their attention spans spanned out and I ended up weaving about 6,000 potholders. I got so good at it that I would be happy to make one for you, provided you send me the $5,000 purchase price in advance.

January 1, 2005

I have been sick through the holidays. The chest and head cold I got last week has hung on and made me miserable. My stomach muscles are weak, which makes it difficult to cough hard enough to get stuff out of my lungs. And the muscle in my left leg hurts all the time; it feels like I have an ice pick stuck in it. Both my hands are getting weaker, but I have better use of my right. I have to develop a new strategy for thumb wars with my grandchildren. Maybe I will change the rules if it looks like I might lose. After all, lawyers are always changing the rules.

What Am I Learning? *It would not come loose. As hard as I tried not to, the tears started to flow. How could I not open a simple little bottle of juice? I was using my good hand, too. My right hand still works most of the time.*

Beth opened it for me. I felt stupid crying about it, but a year and a half ago I was using a ninety-five pound dumbbell with that same right hand.

Lord, this is so hard. Every day I lose something else.
Beth just hugged me.

I used to be so strong. Now I have trouble opening a dumb bottle. And I expect to cry more, God. But I still choose to be thankful. When I choose to mourn and complain, I miss out on the joy God has waiting for me.

For a guy with a fatal disease, I am doing pretty well! I am being fitted for leg braces, which should help keep me from falling down. My hands do not work well, but I still can type better than my dog Lou and my comments are more interesting. My voice still works; I can still eat and, contrary to popular opinion, my brain still works most of the time. Since I have lost about 20 pounds of muscle mass, the doctor has reminded me to eat anything and everything. Sweeter words were never spoken. Would you mind passing the crème brulée?

What Am I Learning? *As I sat watching television the other night, I scratched my chest over my breastbone and was stunned. For the first time I can remember, I felt the ribs in the middle of my chest. That part of my chest has always been covered with strong pectoral muscles. I was shocked to realize those muscles are gone.*

People ask what it feels like to be dying. I say it is strange to see my outward body changing before my eyes. My legs look like toothpicks with calf muscles hanging on the back of little shinbone-

*wide sticks. My thighs are about half what they were. My hands,
which were always strong enough to control another wrestler just by
gripping his wrist, are now hollow and shriveled. My thumbs shake.
My chest has left and my stomach hangs out since the abdominal
muscles are not strong enough to hold it in. My ego is sure taking
a hit.*

*For years I knew my body well and got used to seeing it every
day. Now when I look in the mirror I see someone different. This
guy cannot walk and he has real problems with balance. Sometimes
he is scared. He certainly does not like the idea of not being able to
dress himself, or feed himself or wipe his own nose. He gets embar-
rassed when he thinks that, in time, he will need help to go to the
bathroom.*

*Someday, unless God intervenes, I will be a captive in my own
body. At that time I may even find myself yearning for my new life
in heaven. Someday this body of mine will stop working altogether.*

*Is it scary to be dying? Yes, absolutely. To die is frightening. I
cannot talk to other people who have done it. It is the unknown.
With all of my heart I would like for this to go away. But I am okay.
My life in heaven is assured. Through God's power, my spirit is doing well, even though my body is not. It is well with my soul.*

February 5, 2005

Beth and I are on the road again. We are driving our wheelchair
van to Florida for a couple weeks to visit family and friends. I
have noticed some changes I do not like. I have trouble buttoning my
pants. We might try Velcro® as long as I do not eat too much. It would
be embarrassing to get up from the table after a big meal and have my
pants explode and drop to the floor.

My breathing continues to be of concern. The doctors think
most of the difficulty has to do with my chest cold at Christmas. It
does not seem to be improving, and I have trouble when I first lie
down at night.

On the good side, I got leg braces this week. They are not the most comfortable things, but they may give me enough stability to hit a golf ball. I do not think I will be able to make much of a turn, but anything is an improvement over not being able to play at all.

What Am I Learning? *Her name was Elizabeth Jane Arn, and she was born in Rochester, New York. She is now my wife of thirty-five years, my partner, my lover, my best friend and literally my other half. As I sat in the car today, I teared up when I caught a glimpse of her resting beside me. How is it possible God would bless me with a woman like this? She has been the best thing that ever happened to me, next to meeting Christ. As I watched her today, I thought about what it means to be one with another.*

"For this reason a man will leave his father and mother and be united to his wife, and they will become one flesh." (Genesis 2:24)

Dave asked 200 times; Beth finally said yes

What is Christian marriage supposed to be? Is it really possible to take two people and make them into one?

Beth and I were the first of our group of Young Life friends to marry. We were not only husband and wife, but we were both leaders in the same Young Life club and worked closely together.

We were so young and stupid that we had a high school guy living in our front room and a girl sleeping on a mattress in our kitchen. Our apartment only had three rooms and a bath. Beth and I did it together and we survived. To complicate matters further, fifteen months into our marriage she gave birth to Jeff, and eight days later we moved to Columbus to start Young Life. I worked with high school kids every day while Beth was alone with Jeff all day and many evenings.

We learned that God needed us to be committed to loving him first, then committed to each other and our family. Those relationships would give us the strength we needed to reach out to others. We raised four kids, made lots of mistakes and are still best friends. How is that possible? How is it possible that despite the fact that this has been the hardest year we have ever been through, we both say it has been the best year of our marriage?

You may have heard Beth say that we both have ALS, even if the disease is only resident in my body. The other night I was having trouble breathing. I could not clear my airways and I was struggling. As I looked up from my chair, there was my pal, right with me. I know she was scared and did not know what to do. But she was at my side. When I hurt, she hurts. When she hurts, I hurt. As I got ready to go on this trip, I was having a difficult time physically. Jenny came over to help and she commented to Beth about what she saw: for each of us, our biggest worry was for the other.

This is what marriage is supposed to be. In fact, this is what God wants all our relationships to be. He wants us to put the well-being of others in front of our own. "'Thou shalt love the Lord thy God with all thy heart, and with all thy soul and with all thy mind.' This is the first and great commandment. And there is a second like it: 'Thou shalt love thy neighbor as thyself.'" (Matthew 22:37-39)

God has taught Beth and me many things about living, loving and following him. For years I have watched her open God's Word each day and ask him to lead her and teach her what it means to be a woman of God. From the earliest days of our marriage, she has demonstrated an unbelievable trust and faith in God.

In our first year of marriage some friends, who also were on Young Life staff, had not been paid. The fiscal year was nearly over, and, in those days, there was no such thing as a guaranteed salary. So, at the end of the year if you were still owed money, it was written off. Our boss asked anyone who was able to help to send money. We had $200 in the bank at the time, and our rent was $105. Feeling very proud of my incredible spirituality, I suggested to Beth that we send them $50. After all, that was 25% of our worldly wealth. I knew she would be so proud of being married to such a spiritual giant. I will never forget Beth's reaction. "Send them the whole $200." I could not believe it. How were we going to pay the rent? How were we going to buy groceries? But I also knew Beth would already have prayed about it. If God said to give them the money, he would supply our needs some other way.

Obviously God was trying to teach this young, dumb Pittsburgh kid about trust. We sent the whole $200 and I was scared, but I do not think Beth was. Two days later, when I got our mail, there was an anonymous bank check for $800. It was not a donation to Young Life, but a personal gift to Beth and me. I was flabbergasted, but, as I remember, Beth just smiled.

I always thought I would be healthy, and in our old age, it would be me pushing Beth around in the wheelchair since she has had three knee surgeries. But as we have struggled with this disease and my legs and hands have gotten weaker, she has quietly taken up the tasks that I cannot do, never complaining or even talking about it. Last night, at the hotel, I told her I would try to pick up the suitcase and put it on the stand since her elbow was hurting. I was able to pick it up, but as I swung it onto the stand, my legs gave out and I fell backwards. Beth tried to catch me. We both ended up on the floor against the wall. And the suitcase teetered for a few seconds, then decided to fall on the floor also. Sitting in Beth's arms, there on the floor, we both started to laugh. You can cry or you can laugh. God has taught us joy, so we just shared a great belly laugh.

Beth and I both feel like this has been the best year of our marriage. You might respond that we must have had a really, really bad marriage if this year is the best. The diagnosis of ALS was a devastating event. The thought that our life together may be coming to an end is horrific at best. However, this year has also stripped away many trivial things that get in the way of our relationship. We get to spend more time together than we ever have. And we have grown so much in our relationship with God as we have tried to trust him in everything. We live each day to the fullest, since we do not know what the next day will bring. We do not argue or disagree much because it does not seem very important. There is no time for it.

She has more wrinkles than she used to and rarely does much cheerleading now, but she is still the girl I married in 1969. I just want to let "her works bring her praise at the city gate." (Proverbs 31:31. Also see Proverbs 31:10-12, 25-31.)

Happy Valentine's Day to all of you.

February 15, 2005

Today, when we walked out of the restaurant, it was 85 degrees. How irritating. For the last week and a half, the temperature has stayed between 70 and 74 degrees, averaging out at a room temperature 72. Now, without warning, it has the audacity to go all the way up to 85. Don't you just hate Florida?

Beth and I have noticed on this trip that my voice is getting weaker and gravelly, and we're wondering if this is related to ALS or to one of my medications. When we get home we plan to discuss it with the doctors. I have observed, however, that Beth did not seem nearly as displeased with my silence as I was. She may even be giving me extra doses of medication during my sleep. I saw an Alfred Hitchcock movie like that once.

Totally gray skies, temperatures in the low thirties, a light drizzle and a cutting wind; I know I'm home. After two weeks in Florida with beautiful blue skies, lots of sun and great temperatures, it still feels so good to be back in Columbus.

Today I went to the respiratory doctor to find out what was going on with my voice. He had really good news. I have a raging infection in my throat! The doctor told me that as crazy as it sounds, most of my breathing issues are still related to the chest cold I got in early December.

I fell today when I stepped out the front door to get the paper. I crashed into the door and landed back in the front hall. While I did not hurt myself, this fall convinced me I need to wear my braces a lot more, even if they are uncomfortable.

What Am I Learning? *I have not always walked humbly with my God and I am sure I will continue to struggle with humility in the future. In fact I have always had strong opinions about what I wanted to happen in my life, even to the point of telling God what I thought would work best.*

For example, I could see Beth and me living together, long into our eighties, on a reasonably comfortable retirement income of no less than six figures. We would move out of the "big house" and into a more reasonable upscale condo and, of course, have a small winter home on a golf course in Arizona or Florida. We would downsize to a smaller car and only one van for traveling when we did not fly. Maybe I could write Christian books and speak to Christian groups at warm resort locations. Of course our children would all be perfect, healthy and beautiful, and our grandchildren would all score 2400 on their SATs and graduate from Yale or Harvard. Being committed Christians, we would share some of our money and a little of our time with God, provided it did not interfere with our country club dues or my tee times. After all, I have spent all these years working my butt off. Why would God want me to give up any of that?

Unfortunately, this is not what God seems to be telling us. God is not interested in being our assistant or having a part-time involvement in our lives. He insists on being in charge. Our plans aim for personal grandeur; his plans come in a lowly manger. Our plans tend to bring us momentary praise; his plans always bring eternal glory. Our plans involve no pain; his plans begin on a cross.

As I struggle with this disease, I begin to understand that I am not in charge. As I relinquish control of my life to God, he gently takes over and shows me that his way is the only way to real joy and peace. "Come to me, all of you who are weary and over-burdened, and I will give you rest. Put on my yoke and learn from me. For I am gentle and humble in heart and you will find rest for your souls. For my yoke is easy and my burden is light." (Matthew 11:28-30)

CHAPTER 6

Spring
God Remains the Same

March 6, 2005

Have you ever had a really, really bad day? Let me tell you about my week! Last Monday, I was struggling for breath. My internist did not think it was asthma so he sent me to the hospital. The ER doctors diagnosed a silent heart attack based on "grossly high" enzyme levels. I spent the night in the CICU. It is pretty hard to sleep with a blood pressure cuff going off every 15 minutes, oxygen squirting up my nose, pressure cuffs on my legs pushing blood back to my heart every few seconds, a bed that pressurizes itself every time I move and a vampire from the lab taking blood every two hours. Apparently they thought I would have the "big one" any moment. In the morning, the doctor told me it was a "significant" heart attack.

A subsequent heart catheterization showed my heart was perfect.

The specialists concluded I had an infection in my lungs that did not show up on my multiple chest x-rays and CT scans. After a day and a half on antibiotics, I started to improve. The bad news is the ALS has done damage. My lungs are presently at 59% of normal and my diaphragm is elevated and weaker on the right side. Even so, once I get over the infection I should be able to breathe reasonably, but my days of cross-country running are definitely over. Most of the cross-country runners I know can also stand up, so I guess they were already over before the breathing problems.

What Am I Learning? *Even in the semi-darkness, it was easy to make out the hands of the clock on the wall. It was broken and, after twenty minutes of the minute hand struggling up the clock face, it would lose its battle with gravity and fall back to the six. I was stuck in a twenty-minute cycle; the time was always between six thirty and six fifty. People came in often to take blood or read monitors, but I was alone in the CICU with my thoughts.*

I guess I really am dying. I thought I had at least another year or two, but with ALS and significant heart damage, how long can I go? What are you doing, Lord? Are you offering me an out, so that I can die of a massive heart attack instead of suffocating from ALS? My life and future rest totally in your hands. I might not see Beth or the kids again. Is tonight it? What will it be like, Lord? Please hold me close, God. This is scary.

"And we rejoice in the hope of the glory of God. Not only so, but we also rejoice in our sufferings, because we know that suffering produces perseverance; perseverance, character; and character, hope. And hope does not disappoint us, because God has poured out his love into our hearts by the Holy Spirit, whom he has given us." (Romans 5:2b-5)

When I was lying in that bed in the hospital, I begged God to take the suffering away. I pleaded with God to ease my breathing. Yet I believe God let my suffering go deeper so I could learn to trust his character and make it part of my character.

At one point in my hospital stay, the doctors decided to do a CT scan of my chest requiring me to lie on my back, the position in which I have the most difficulty breathing. To make matters worse, they required me to hold my arms over my head and to hold my breath. I was on the verge of total panic. It was the worst thing they had done to me.

I had only been back to my room for five minutes when they came to tell me that they had to do the test over. I panicked. How could I do it again? I had barely survived the first time. Beth and I held hands and prayed.

God, just calm me down and go with me. Let me breathe without fear.

When they put me back in the machine, I did better. My breathing was labored, but much calmer than before. I was all right and, once again, I learned God is trustworthy. If I can trust him for breath, lying on my back in a CT scanner, can I not trust him with everything else?

As Beth and I suffer through this disease, I can rejoice, not because I like to suffer in some sick way, but because I am slowly discovering God is absolutely true to his word and promises.

Perseverance has produced a character change. It is not that I am anything special. The truth is I know how weak and self-centered I am. But as I turn more of my life over to God, he produces a solid hope that will carry me through adversities.

March 16, 2005

When I got out of the hospital last week, my breathing was improved. This week, without the antibiotics, my breathing difficulties quickly returned. My doctor told me to go back on another course of antibiotics. This infection is being difficult and does not want to give up its hold on my bronchial tubes.

Physically I'm a mess right now. Even so, not to worry. I maintain those rugged good looks that so many of you have come to expect from me. On top of that, my hair is still not gray, so I've got that going for me, too. Maybe I can get the doctors to save my hair and just get a total body transplant of everything under my hair.

March 24, 2005

This has been a difficult time. Every time I got to the end of my antibiotics, the labored breathing returned. Following four courses of antibiotics, we went back to the pulmonary doctor to see why the antibiotics were not finishing the job. After several tests, he advised us the ALS has done significant damage to my diaphragm. My ability to breathe changes by 40% when I lie down. My diaphragm is damaged and, because of the ALS, it will not get better. The lower parts of my lungs have collapsed and collect the fluids my body cannot eliminate, leaving a breeding ground for infection. Since the ALS is irreversible, the next step is some mechanical means to help clear my lungs: a breathing machine to help at night and a special machine that vibrates my lungs to clear the phlegm.

The disease is more advanced than we had hoped. The diaphragm problem and respiratory difficulties are usually what kill you with ALS. We had hoped to face these issues further down the road.

I do not yet need a respirator to breathe for me. Of course, absent God's miraculous intervention, that will be the option some day. I do not like the idea of living on a respirator. We will certainly need God's help to make that decision. And God can be trusted in all things, even those things we fear the most.

April 1, 2005

We have actually had a couple of wonderful sunny days in Columbus. I felt good enough that Beth and I took a long walk on the bicycle trails through the park; she walked and I took a borrowed power wheelchair since mine has not yet arrived. I would have preferred to walk, but it was absolutely wonderful to get outside. I am pretty fast in that chair. Every time we came to an intersection, I looked for someone to race. Too bad I cannot rev the engine or make it louder by taking off the muffler. Battery power is just so boring.

I am on my sixth course of antibiotics and take three or four breathing treatments a day. I am breathing a little easier.

D o you know the toughest ticket to get in all sports? It is Sunday at the Masters in Augusta, Georgia. I am telling you that little tidbit because my neighbor gave my son Jeff and me tickets. After the Young Life 35th Anniversary Celebration tonight, we fly early Sunday to Atlanta and then drive to Augusta. I will be tired, but who cares. It is the Masters.

What Am I Learning? *This weekend I spoke at the Columbus Young Life 35th Anniversary Banquet. There were at least 400 Young Life folks from the past there, and we got to be the honored guests. Jenny sang a song she wrote for us, and our sons Jeff, Mike and Andy were all in skits poking fun at the ministry and those of us in it. What a great night! I thought you might enjoy reading my talk for the evening:*

It is good to be with you as we celebrate the amazing work God has done here in Columbus through all of us, and in a lot of ways in spite of us. I cannot tell you how funny it feels to think that it has been 35 years.

In the book of Judges, we find the very interesting story of Israel and its enemy the Midianites. The Midianites had so oppressed and overrun the Jews that scripture says they had nothing. The Midianite raiders would sweep in and steal every crop, animal and valuable of the Israelites, leaving them no option but to hide in caves. In the sixth chapter, we meet Gideon. He, like everyone else, is hiding, threshing wheat inside a wine press so that the Midianites will not find him and steal the wheat. An angel of the Lord approaches Gideon there and tells him, "The Lord is with you, mighty warrior." He responds like most of us would. "But sir," Gideon replies, "If the Lord is with us, why has all this happened to us? Where are all the signs and wonders that our fathers told us about...?" In other words, "Are you kidding me? How can I trust that God is helping? With friends like that, who needs enemies? If this is the way you are going to help us, how bad could it be if you weren't?" Gideon is told to go with the strength he has to defeat the Midianites. "But Lord," Gideon asks, "how can I save Israel? My clan is the weakest in Manasseh, and I am the least of my family."

Gideon is like many of us. Notice that God calls him a "mighty warrior," but Gideon does not believe God and thinks of himself as "the least of my family." He thinks in human terms, not realizing that he worships the very God of the Universe. Gideon is scared and nervous, but through some tests the Lord proves to Gideon that he is trustworthy. Then comes the really fascinating part of the story. Gideon assembles his troops, 32,000 of them. Meanwhile, it is impossible to count the Midianites; they are as numerous as locusts. Then the Lord says something unbelievable to Gideon, "You have too many men for me to deliver Midian into your hands." Can you imagine Gideon's response? "Did you say, 'Too many men?' You've got to be kidding me." But God tells Gideon that if they go into battle with all these men, the Israelites will think they won on their own strength. So Gideon is told to send away everyone who is afraid. Twenty-two thousand go home. Gideon now has 10,000 warriors left. And what does God do? He tells Gideon he still has too many men, and that he should pare his force down further. Finally when Gideon has only 300 men, God tells him it is just right.

To man, this makes no sense, yet we know the rest of the story. Gideon and his 300 men defeated an army of at least 135,000 men. How is that possible?

"But God chose the foolish things of the world to shame the wise; God chose the weak things of the world to shame the strong. He chose the lowly things of this world and the despised things – and the things that are not – to nullify the things that are, so that no one may boast before him. It is because of him that you are in Christ Jesus, who has become for us wisdom from God – that is, our righteousness, holiness and redemption. Therefore, as it is written, 'Let him who boasts, boast in the Lord.'" (1 Corinthians 1:27-31)

When God chose to start Young Life in Columbus, Ohio, you

might have thought he would call a seasoned, proven leader with significant experience in starting a ministry and mission from scratch. Instead he chose a 22-year-old kid, only one year out of college, with no experience at anything beyond a few feeble attempts at listening to God. You might have thought he would have provided significant financial support for that ministry. Instead he sent a young couple with an eight-day-old baby and no visible means of support. And you might have thought that he would provide easy access to high school kids. Instead, this rookie was not allowed on the campus of the high school where he believed God wanted him to start. Sounds like the story of Gideon all over again.

Millions of Young Life memories, like this one with Dave and Bev (Brown) DeLashmutt

But my boss had told me to get kids to go to Frontier Ranch in Colorado so we would have a group to start Young Life in the fall.

Since the principal had told me I was not allowed at the school, I stood across the street by the fireplug with all the neighborhood dogs. As the kids crossed, I struck up conversations with them. "Hey, kid. Want to go to Colorado? By the way, that dog is peeing on your leg." I told them I didn't live here – that I was only in town for two weeks and didn't even have a local phone number – but if they gave me a $25 deposit I would be back in a month with a big bus and *take them to Colorado. Every evening I met with different kids' parents and tried to convince them they should let their kids go.*

What do you suppose I was able to do?

Nothing.

But God was able to get 45 kids signed up. When I returned one month later, everyone showed up to go to Frontier and over half of those kids made commitments to Christ at camp. With that miracle of God, we started Young Life in Columbus in September 1970. By the end of the school year, we had clubs in three schools and over 400 kids at our all-city Young Life club.

In the beginning, Beth and I had no other leaders to work with, but God took care of that. I wore a Young Life sweatshirt to The Ohio State University Student Union and quickly met a number of students who had been in Young Life in other cities. From that group, God called a small number of folks who loved the Lord and were willing to hang out with high school kids when they were not in class. Please understand, we did not pull this off. God did. There was no leadership program those first couple years; we prayed a lot and experimented. By 1979, we had enough leadership to work in thirteen schools.

Now Young Life here is in twenty-five high schools! Next fall, when all those clubs are really cranking, there will be over 2,000 kids a week hearing the Gospel. This summer, about 700 kids from this area will go to Young Life camp with our awesome leaders. On their own, it will be impossible for these leaders to reach this teenage population even if they are the most talented people in the world. That is because this is a work of God and not of us. He will do marvelous things. He is the God who can take the heart of a 16- or 17-year-old kid and change his life forever.

On a more personal level, God has demonstrated his character to Beth and me for years. He has cared for us, loved us, worked with us and used us in amazing ways. On October 28, 2003, I was diagnosed with ALS, Lou Gehrig's disease. It was a devastating diagnosis that hit us right between the eyes. I have always been healthy and active and now we were being told that over time I would become a quadriplegic and within one to five years would die of respiratory failure. How was that supposed to help the Kingdom of God?

Over the years, Beth and I have discovered that God's character remains the same. He is always trustworthy and ready to help us when we seek him. He has been there for us when we had no money, during times of great spiritual growth and great spiritual famine, in times of sinful neglect and pride, and every other moment of our lives. He may not have met our needs the way we would have liked, but he was always faithful and was always there for us. His character is unchanging.

But what about the future?

Since I was a small child with asthma, the one thing that has really frightened me is the fear of not being able to breathe. While my ALS is progressing slowly, three and a half months ago I began to have significant trouble breathing. It got progressively worse; I was hospitalized, and learned my diaphragm is damaged, with only about 50% lung function. We had hoped the respiratory problems would come later, yet here they are.

*This has caused us to turn to God with our fears: **"God, I do not know if I can do this."***

His reply is no surprise, "You can't! But I can."

I am coming to know even more of the character of God. He loves me and cares for me and my family more than we can ever know or understand. He has promised all things fit together for good for those that love the Lord. His character is to be trusted.

Sometimes God is glorified by changing our circumstances, and sometimes God is glorified by changing us in our circumstances. Both are true, yet God always remains unchangeable. His character in the past will be his character in the future. "Jesus Christ is always the same, yesterday, today and forever." (Hebrews 13:8)

As I contemplate my future, I can easily recall times when God has been glorified by changing our circumstances, such as when he moved us to Columbus to start Young Life. And we have already seen ways in which he is using this illness to bring glory to himself and his kingdom by impacting not only our lives and faith, but also the lives and faith of family, friends and even people we do not know. I am so blessed by God to see him work in this way.

Despite all this, I get frightened as I contemplate my future. What will it be like not to be able to breathe? How can I deal with the panic? How do I face something that frightening? I do not have an easy answer, but God has loved me and cared for me in the past, and he has loved me and cared for me over the eighteen months since my diagnosis. Why would he not continue to love me and care for me through the end of my life here on earth? Since God's character remains the same, can I not trust such a God to love me and care for me no matter what my circumstances? As we approach this difficult future, can we not trust the love of such a God in all things, even the horribly frightening? "Yet the Lord is utterly to be depended upon by all who have faith in him, and he will give you stability and protection against all that is evil." (2 Thessalonians 3:3)

I will not tell you I am not afraid. Who is crazy enough to want to suffer? Even our Lord asked in the Garden if he had to go through with death on the cross. Yet Jesus did willingly go to the cross because he knew the character of the Father and he was willing to trust everything to him.

To be honest, I am scared to death. Yet I know my God and he loves me. Has the God who gave Gideon the victory changed? Has the character of the one who miraculously put 45 kids on a bus to Colorado changed? Will the Lord, who tenderly embraced children, now forget his child, David? No! He is the same yesterday, today and tomorrow. His character is always to be trusted and he has promised he will be with me forever.

I do not know the direction my future will go, but I do know with whom I will be going. He is sufficient for all I need and he will lead me with his sure hand. What more can I ask?

We have asked and answered a number of questions about God tonight, but we cannot leave here without asking the question: who *is God to you? Are you willing to trust God with all those things that frighten you? Is Jesus Christ your Savior and the Lord of your life? If you have never asked Jesus into your heart, you have no idea what you are missing. To truly know the love, care and forgiveness of Christ, you must open your heart to him. If you have never done that, in a minute when we pray, please invite him into your heart. If you have previously asked Jesus in, please ask yourself if you are living your life trusting in God and his unchanging character. Man thinks he knows how to live, but it is not until we truly allow God to live in us that we experience real living. "But if on the other hand you cut the nerve of your instinctive actions by obeying the Spirit, you are on the way to real living." (Romans 8:13)*

Who will God be in the future? He will be the same. He will be the Alpha and the Omega, the Beginning and the End, the Mighty God, the Prince of Peace, the Lamb of God, the Light of the World, the Author of Truth, the God above all Gods, the God of Ages, the Fullness of Grace, the Creator of the Universe. And he will be all we need in every situation, the same yesterday, today and tomorrow.

Dave delivers the keynote at the Columbus Young Life 35th Anniversary Banquet

The weather in Columbus has been wonderful. Saturday, Beth and I went to three of five grandkids' soccer games. Abby and Rinnah played at 8:30 a.m. That was too early for me, but we made Claire's game at 11:00, Rachael's game at 12:00 and Kayley's game at 5:30. I am beginning to wonder what we will do with nine grandkids when they all play a sport. Who says retirement is easy?

I got a breathing machine for sleeping. It is called a BiPAP and is similar to the device people with sleep apnea use. It has high pressure when I breathe in to force air into my lungs and low pressure when I breathe out to allow my damaged diaphragm to get the CO_2 out of my system, so I have been sleeping much better. The downside is I have this mask and hose covering my face at night. I look like Darth Vader. Beth is not scared, but I wonder what the grandkids would do if they saw me. Don't you just hate it when your grandkids see you and run screaming from the room?

Walking back from one of the soccer games, I stepped into a small depression and went down hard, even with my braces and my cane. I was wearing shorts and got grass stains on my braces. Maybe when people see the grass stains, they will think I am still playing contact sports. Is walking a contact sport? It must be.

What Am I Learning? *It was 1960. I was breathing heavily and had my head down when the golf ball almost hit me. I quickly looked up the hill to see a kid hitting golf balls with a baseball bat. After a couple hits, the bat snapped, and the kid hurled it down the hill and went inside to get another bat. A minute later he was back out there hitting golf balls.*

I picked up the pieces of the bat he had thrown and was shocked as I read the label. It was a Louisville Slugger, Genuine Dick Stuart Original. This was not just any bat, but an actual bat used by the Pirate's first baseman, Dick Stuart, and this kid had broken it and thrown it away. What was wrong with this guy?

When I got to the top of the hill, I introduced myself and asked if I could have the broken bat.

"Sure," he replied, "but wouldn't you rather have one that's not broken?"

He took me in his garage and showed me a barrel full of bats. Each one was a treasure. There were Roberto Clemente bats, Dick Groat bats, Bill Verdon bats, Bill Mazeroski bats and many more, all originals. What was going on?

This new kid was Donnie Brown, son of the Pittsburgh Pirates General Manager, Joe Brown. We became fast friends. As a sports fanatic growing up in Pittsburgh in the sixties, I only dreamed of meeting some of my baseball heroes. With Donnie as my friend, I met everybody. I met most of the Pirates and even got to spend an entire afternoon with Casey Stengel, the Baseball Hall of Fame manager of the Yankees when the Pirates were in the World Series. One summer I went to 59 home games as the guest of the Pirates, sitting in the press box and eating meal after meal on the team. I would love to tell you that all those people were my friends and spent time with me because I was such a great guy, but the truth is it all came about because I knew Donnie Brown.

Sometimes, we think we receive blessings because we are such great people. Actually it has little to do with us, but everything to do with whom we know, Jesus Christ. Once I knew Jesus, I experienced and accomplished more in this life than I ever dared dream or imagine, not because I was special, but because I knew him.

May 5, 2005

What Am I Learning? *I was home alone. I had shaved, brushed my teeth and worked myself in and out of the shower. Getting up, medicating myself and getting dressed takes an arduous hour and a half. When people ask me out for breakfast, I tell them, "Sure, as long as breakfast is at 11:00 a.m." Having finished my shower, I sat contemplating my favorite pair of jeans. The next task was to get my legs down through my pants, which*

I did without getting my toes hung up! I pushed myself up on the arms of the chair and stood to pull the pants up. Since I did not have my braces on yet, I hung onto shelves and leaned the backs of my legs against the chair, which I had pushed against the wall so it would not move. I let go with one hand and swung myself forward so the backs of my legs cleared the chair. Timing was everything. If I was lucky and did not fall, I could then lean against the wall to button them and fasten my belt.

But try as I might, I could not get the button through the hole. I quickly got winded and had to sit down to rest. After three periods of multiple attempts, I was so tired I had to give up. I started to cry.

Lord, it's too hard. How am I supposed to do this?

I finally quit crying, not because I felt better, but because when I cry, it is harder to breathe. After 30 minutes, I changed into sweatpants with an elastic waist. Obviously, my days as a fashion model for Gentlemen's Quarterly *are over.*

It is rarely the big things that make living with ALS difficult. Instead, it's the little things, like buttoning my pants, that get to me. I recognize as this horrible disease progresses I will suffer losses, and the little things bring this realization into focus. I cannot do most buttons. It is hard to cut meat and use a fork because the utensils slide through my fingers. So, when I hold my fork with my fingers like a fist, do people assume I have no manners whatsoever? When I keep making violent noises trying to clear my throat because it is difficult to cough, do people just assume I am rude and untrained?

When I was able-bodied, I never realized how emotionally difficult it is to be physically unable to do the simplest tasks. As I try to be God's man, I struggle against feeling sorry for myself. I seem to understand the big picture, the life and death issues. But when I wrestle with daily tasks, I forget what God has taught me. I need to be careful to keep the little things in perspective and not allow them to become overwhelming.

What Am I Learning? *Today, it struck me. It was one of those light-bulb moments when I clearly saw something God was saying to me.*

One of the reasons I am sick is that God wants to use me.

I broke down and cried. More than anything in my life, I have wanted to be God's man and respond to his call.

I can point to three previous times when I believe God made calls on my life: in 1968 when I graduated from college and knew God wanted me to work for Young Life; when we moved to Columbus in 1970 to start the work here; and when, after ten years with Young Life, God called me to return to school and enter the practice of law.

Is ALS God's new call on our lives? I know he is once again asking me to trust and follow him.

Why would he need me to be sick for this call? Because, as I have told many people, nobody tells a dying guy to shut up.

CHAPTER 7

Summer
Stop Long Enough to Look

<hr>

June 15, 2005

Yesterday was our 36th anniversary. To celebrate we went on a cruise. It is awesome when your lover of thirty-six years is sensitive to your every need. On the first night, Beth wheeled me to our room and left to see a movie with the family. I got myself medicated and in bed by 10:00, leaving a reading light on for Beth. Much later, when she decided to turn in, she tried to turn off the reading light, but only succeeded in turning on every light in the room, trying switch after switch. Next she opened the drapes twice with the motorized opener, which ground away with a rather loud and obnoxious sound. Finally, as if this had not been enough to get me wide-awake, she hit the only remaining switch, which was the emergency call button for our handicapped room. Immediately the phone rang. I told the medical personnel, "No I do not have an emergency. I am all right, but my wife would like to know how to turn off the reading light."

What Am I Learning? *The fierce and deadly battle within my body rages on and on. In the beginning, the enemy had thrust and probed around the perimeter, looking for any weakness. When found, it attacked with a vengeance rarely seen. Though the* fighting intensified, it was hard to sense what was happening, except at night. It was at night, in those stretches of darkness, when I heard the cries of the wounded. "Help me, I am dying. Won't you please help me?" But there was nothing I could do. How could I help? In the morning there were no more sounds, no cries. And I knew they were gone, of no further use to me. They were dead. But I simply had to go on.

I remember the early skirmishes, before I really knew we were at war. I was weak and it was at night when I felt them, those little twitches in my muscles. I had sensed them before, but never like this. So many of them and they kept coming. It was there, in the dark, when I first had the courage to count them, all over my body, those little twitches. When I realized that there were 60 to 80 of them a minute, I was stunned. Part of me was wounded and I was in trouble. The worst were in my legs. As they increased in severity, my legs got weaker and weaker, until they were gone. They were dead to me below the knee. And I had to forget about them, for the battle raged. Little time to mourn the losses, the fasciculations were now waging war for my hands and thighs. Soon another new front opened and my lungs were at risk.

Lord, how is this possible that I am dying a little bit at a time? This disease is taking no prisoners.

As I lay in bed, I could feel the latest, devastating attacks. There were deep, deep fasciculations in my chest and abdomen. Those are the ones that do not just rob you. They are the ones that kill. Not just the limbs, but me.

God, I am in such trouble. I need you here with me on this. All my life I have been a fighter. I have always known how to win. But how do I win at this?

It was dark in the room, but it got lighter as it dawned on me. I was not supposed to fight this battle alone.

Beth and I still have a life. We depend on God for it, and we are so much more appreciative of it. The suffering matters less, for God loves us and he is using us to his glory. We are happy to have *another day together. What joy and pleasure we experience. What sweetness we know.*

So, each night, Beth helps me out of my leg braces. I put on my BiPAP mask with the long hose that makes me look like a character out of Star Wars™ and literally crawl into bed.

"Good night, Beth."

"Good night, Darth."

July 3, 2005

Have you ever had a week that was so bad you wanted to scratch it off the calendar? I spent most of the week in my chair hooked to my breathing machine. When the heat and humidity dropped Saturday, Beth and I decided it was time to have some fun, so we went to Picnic with the Pops. It is supposed to be a great evening outside with 15,000 of your closest friends picnicking and listening to the Columbus Symphony Orchestra. While we enjoy the symphony, we are not jazz fans. The evening included a jazz ensemble playing with the orchestra, but we assumed, since the program was to be patriotic numbers, the jazz part would be small. What an evening!

When we arrived, we discovered that my wheelchair battery was dead. Then I choked on my food and hacked and retched long enough to draw the attention and ruin the appetite of about 10,000 of the 15,000 people there. Beth lit sparklers for us to wave to the music. With my bad thumb, I dropped one onto my lap and burned a hole right through my new jacket.

After only two symphony pieces, the jazz band took over for the orchestra and played on and on and on. It has long been my opinion that piping mandatory jazz into all prison cells would significantly cut down on repeat offenders. As the program drew to a close, even *Stars and Stripes Forever* was unrecognizable with its syncopated beat. The culmination of the evening came when the concluding fireworks were launched directly behind the building looming right in front of us. We tried to match the crowd and time our "Oohs" and "Ahs" with what we thought might be happening behind the building.

Hope your week was better.

This Thursday, the Muscular Dystrophy Association is honoring me at the Columbus Clippers baseball game. I am to receive their "Personal Achievement Award." WSYX/ABC 6 is interviewing me, and I will appear on the news and on the Jerry Lewis Telethon in September. I hope I have an opportunity to share about Christ.

Abby, Claire, Kayley, Kirsten and their Papa watch as an MDA representative introduces Dave for Yolanda Harris, WSYX/ABC 6, Columbus

What Am I Learning? *"I cry aloud to the Lord; I lift up my voice to the Lord for mercy. I pour out my complaint before him; before him I tell my trouble. When my spirit grows faint within me, it is you who know my way." (Psalm 142:1-3a)*

What is it you want of me, Lord? How do I live each day now? How can I lift you up so you can draw others to you?

All this last week I spent in my chair. I felt so poorly, that I simply wanted to sit there. While Beth and I went out a few times to dinner with friends or family, when I got back, I was wiped out. When I spoke at church last week, it took everything I had just to get the words out.

Is this really what you want of me?

"But he said to me, 'My grace is sufficient for you, for my power is made perfect in weakness.' Therefore I will boast all the more gladly about my weakness, so that Christ's power may rest on me. That is why, for Christ's sake, I delight in weakness, in insults, in hardships, in persecution, in difficulties. For when I am weak, then I am strong." (2 Corinthians 12:9-10)

You know how weak I am, Lord.

I used to be a good attorney. I was known for being creative and a good problem solver. Now I just sit. I just signed my license renewal form for the Supreme Court and checked "inactive." I am no longer licensed to practice law. The world has passed me by. I am physically unable to do most everything I used to find easy. Now I just sit. I used to be so active in every kind of endeavor. Now I just sit.

Yet when I work to breathe, you are here. When I struggle to walk, you are here. When I fall on my face, you are here. You give me breath and you carry me and you pick me up. At night, when I am alone and weak, you are here and we talk. To you be all glory and honor, for it is in you only that I find my strength. For you, Oh Lord, have been there before me. I believe in your Son, Jesus. You gave up your Son and he allowed himself to suffer and die, so that I could be yours and live with you forever. If you loved me enough to allow that, surely you are with me now. You comfort me with your love and care every minute of the day. Thank you, Lord.

"I cry to you, O Lord; I say, 'You are my refuge, my portion in the land of the living.' Listen to my cry, for I am in desperate need; rescue me from those who pursue me, for they are too strong for me. Set me free from my prison, that I may praise your name." (Psalm 142:5-7a)

Lord, I am suffering. But you know that. I am in desperate need. You know that, too. Lord, I am in prison. But you know that also. Lord, you know everything about me, for you are right here with me every minute of every day and you love me. You know that I cannot breathe. You know that I cannot walk. You know that I cannot dress myself. May you use every ounce of my suffering to bring you glory. May you use my weakness to bring others to understand how awesome is your grace and your forgiveness.

"Praise the Lord. Praise the Lord, O my soul. I will praise the Lord all my life; I will sing praise to my God as long as I live. Do not put your trust in princes, in mortal men, who cannot save. When their spirit departs, they return to the ground; on that very day their plans come to nothing. Blessed is he whose help is the God of Jacob, whose hope is in the Lord his God, the Maker of heaven and earth, the sea, and everything in them – the Lord who remains faithful forever. He upholds the cause of the oppressed and gives food to the hungry. The Lord sets prisoners free, the Lord gives sight to the blind, the Lord lifts up those who are bowed down, the Lord loves the righteous. The Lord watches over the alien and sustains the fatherless and the widow, but he frustrates the ways of the wicked. The Lord reigns forever, your God, O Zion, for all generations. Praise the Lord." (Psalm 146)

Praise you, Lord, for each breath I take. Praise you, Lord, for your Son, Jesus the Christ. I am yours, Lord. Comfort me in my suffering and give me rest, both now and when the race is won.

July 28, 2005

I had a wonderful five days with my two brothers, Ed and Bob. We bought an 18-year-old RV really cheap and traveled to Oshkosh, Wisconsin, for the world's largest air show. At the Experimental Aircraft Association's annual Air Venture, we overdosed on thousands of airplanes of every description, including home-builts, antiques and war birds. It was a great opportunity to be together and enjoy something our wives would hate. Ed and Bob took good care of me, and my power wheelchair performed amazingly well as we covered miles and miles of airplane mania. The big advantage I had is that they had all the responsibility. Since this RV is so old, and since we paid almost nothing for it, it required the efforts of both brilliant engineer-type brothers to keep everything running. I successfully avoided anything resembling work, and fortunately they did not complain.

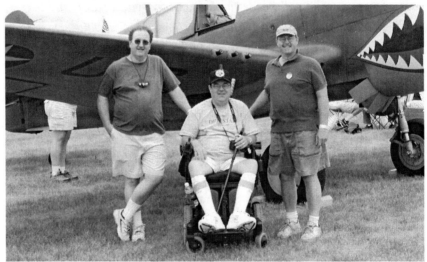

The Chilcoat brothers (L to R): Ed, Dave and Bob at the EAA Fly-In, Oshkosh, WI

What Am I Learning? *My friend Betsy died Sunday night. She passed away peacefully after a one-year struggle with ALS. Beth and I got to see her the day before she died. She was smiling and happy to be surrounded by her husband and family. We got to read some scriptures to her and tell her we loved her. She told us she loved us, too.*

We met Betsy through my website journal. One day she called and we talked about being sick, belonging to Christ and suffering. Over time we became friends. She was a wonderful artist who had a gallery in the Short North. She once told me that at night, when she felt bad and could not sleep, she read my website over and over again. Betsy thought God's Word was beautiful and found comfort there. I cried when I heard she died. I will miss her.

August 5, 2005

I did well this week at Hilton Head.

The youngest Chilcoat cousins (L to R), Owen, Toby and Kendal at Hilton Head

I stayed inside most of the time, except for short forays to the pool, boat rides or restaurants. I was even able to stay outside and watch six of our little granddaughters sing at the Greg Russell concert at the harbor one evening.

One night I went to bed early and had difficulty breathing. I had to call Beth, who was hanging out with the kids in another unit. Before I knew it, half the family was in my bedroom trying to help. I never thought breathing would become a family affair.

I have begun to experience some trouble with my neck muscles, the equivalent of a stiff, sore neck. I may require a neck collar, which does not sound good. I am guessing people will just assume it is because, as an attorney, my head has gotten so big that I need help holding it up.

What Am I Learning? *I sat at the corner of the table and watched, my beautiful wife beside me. Around the table sat my wonderful children, their terrific spouses and all nine of our precious grandchildren. How awesome to have all of us together. It was difficult to get the kids settled beside the specific cousin each wanted. After a little chaos, things settled down. I sat there taking it all in. How could anyone be more blessed? How could anyone want more out of life?*

Then I started to cry. I do not want to leave them. I do not want to die. It was a wonderful night and a lousy night.

As we have vacationed here at Hilton Head, we have seen the incredible creativity of our God, from the sandpipers hopping along the beach on one leg to the beauty of the sunset over the water and the dolphins cruising beside the boat in the shallow inlet. The variety and magnificence of God's creation is all around us. If we stop long enough to look, we see the majesty of a Creator who entertains us at every turn. How amazing it will be to live with God for eternity and experience first hand the essence of his creativity!

I have so many questions. Why did he make toadstools and roaches and what is it with armadillos? How come lobsters are so ugly and yet taste so good? Did he really expect us to eat them? Why do flounder have both eyes on the same side of their heads? Why didn't I get a hyperactive thyroid gland so I could eat without worrying about getting fat and why do wives get headaches? If this world we see, with all its incredible beauty and creativity, was fashioned by God, how much more amazing will heaven be? If this life, damaged as it is by man's sin and ego, is still attractive, how much more astonishing and inviting will it be to live with God without sin and evil?

God has allowed me to see the wonder of the births of my four children. He has allowed me to see the grandeur of the Grand Canyon, the Rocky Mountains and the Alps. God has let me bask in the beauty of the Caribbean Sea, the wonder of watching an impressive array of stars on a cloudless night in Colorado and the power of hundreds of breaching whales in Maui. I have had the incredible opportunity of watching grandchildren splashing in the waves at the beach and catching fireflies on a still summer evening. No, I do not want to leave this world.

But I choose to believe that the same God who has given me a glimmer of his creativity here, the same God who has amazed me with his majesty and his creation, will keep his promise of a place prepared for me in heaven, designed and executed by the mighty author of the universe. The God that loves, comforts and amazes me here will also love, comfort and amaze me for eternity. And he will keep my family in his sure grip.

August 13, 2005

I am not completely worthless. I just took the car and rescued Beth and Andy who were on a bike ride and got caught in the rain and lightning. ALS Guy to the rescue in his amazing wheelchair-equipped sports van. Able to leap tall buildings in a single... Sorry, I got carried away.

What Am I Learning? *"...then choose for yourselves this day whom you will serve, whether the gods your forefathers served beyond the River, or the gods of the Amorites, in whose land you are living. But as for me and my household, we will serve the Lord." (Joshua 24:15)*

This is a wonderful passage of scripture, for it calls us to make a real, honest decision about whom we will believe and serve. It is as relevant today as it was for Joshua in the Old Testament.

In June 1962, at Young Life's Frontier Ranch, I made my choice and asked Jesus to live in my heart. On that night in Colorado, I forever settled the question of eternity for me. In 1965, I entered the University of Pittsburgh as a cocky, wild young man. I knew Jesus and had made a commitment to him, but frankly, I did not want to live the way he wanted me to live. I was much more interested in partying and experimenting with booze and girls. It took two years of fleeing from God before I was willing to actually let him run my life. Sitting in my underwear, watching Johnny Carson late at night, I was lonely and unhappy. The life I had been living was not pleasing to God. I was miserable, not because my carousing was not working, but because inside me, God's Holy Spirit had taken up residence and was constantly reminding me I was supposed to be living for God and not myself. That night, I chose to let God be the Lord of my life.

This last week was a difficult one. I walked out of a restroom at a highway rest area and Beth helped me back to the car. As I stepped down over the curb, I fell straight down to the concrete. I managed to bounce the back of my head so hard, the front of my brain hurt. A crowd quickly gathered to help. Then more than my head hurt; my pride was damaged. As I prayed about it, I realized my challenge was to choose to believe God, that his power is made perfect in weakness.

Wednesday, I had surgery to place a feeding tube in my stomach. I did not want it. Who wants a twelve-inch hunk of latex tubing sticking out of the middle of your abdomen? (I have come up with some really good jokes about it, but Beth will not let me use any of them.)

I hate the tube and I hate what it means. Only two years ago, I was healthy. In the past I might have given you pat spiritual answers about why some people suffer, but those responses have been swallowed up by useless legs and fumbling hands. I used to brim with optimism about life, because I had so much confidence in me and I believed there was little I could not do. Now that confidence has been undermined by lungs that do not work and a latex tube in my belly.

It is easy to choose God and follow him when we are experiencing prosperity and plenty. It is easy to give glory to God when our life is full, when everything we touch looks perfect, in a day of strength or during a mountain top experience when blessings rain down, when success is plentiful and status quo is assumed or when years stretch before you like future rewards for a job well done. On those days it is easy to choose God. But what about when the world around us is falling apart? When we are struggling and nothing is going right, we begin to understand how difficult it can be to choose to allow God to reign. That choice cannot be based upon circumstances or emotions. God is either true or he is a liar. The Bible either says the truth or it is a fairy tale. If God is true in the light, he must be true in the darkness. If he is true in strength, he must be true in weakness. He wants me to choose whom I will serve. As for me and my household, we choose this day to serve the Lord.

CHAPTER 8

Fall
Fixing My Eyes on the Unseen

September 16, 2005

Monday, Beth and I and our dog Lou are heading to Florida to visit Beth's mom and brother. Today the respiratory specialist told me my breathing capacity has diminished to 43% in the last three months. That's a drop of about 6%, which cannot be good. As long as the weather is not too hot and humid (great time to head to Florida, eh?), and as long as I do all my breathing treatments, I seem to do all right.

October 3, 2005

Beth and I are back from Florida and I am writing this journal entry by using my new voice-activated software. Even though I am not quite used to it yet, it makes fewer mistakes than my fingers.

What Am I Learning? *We always use the handicapped van now. And, after my latest face plant on the concrete on our trip to Florida, Beth and I have decided to retire the cane. Depending on the cane was like trying to balance on the head of a pin, and Beth was not strong enough to hold me up when I started to fall.*

That leaves us with a difficult decision when it comes to long trips. Since the doctors insist I drink a lot of water to stay hydrated, I never see a rest area I do not like. Upon arriving at one, we have to decide between using the wheelchair or the walker.

Initially the power wheelchair seemed to be the best option, but using it necessitated first removing everything that was packed on top of it, such as the shower chair, the bottled water, the wheelchair charger, the chest vibration machine, my standard nebulizer, my BiPAP machine and miscellaneous other survival items. Next we had to remove the dog, the dog's food and water, and the dog's cage in order to have room to maneuver. Finally, we had to unstrap the wheelchair, lower the ramp and wheel out the chair. This process took no less than 32½ minutes. Upon finishing my visit to the restroom, we had to reverse the process. With Beth doing all the heavy lifting in 95° heat, she also considered taking advantage of truckers' showers at our gas stops. This whole approach seemed impractical, however, since it would take us three weeks to get to Florida. Accordingly, we decided to use the walker.

Walkers were originally created as instruments of torture by first century B.C. Roman centurions. They are misnamed; neither the device nor its user can walk.

My walker has wheels on the front two legs and plastics skids with springs on the back legs. The idea is that you roll easily forward and, when you need to stop, you simply press down on the back legs; then the springs will bend and the feet will contact the ground. That's the theory anyway. Nothing slides easily along concrete, asphalt, brick, dirt and other roadway materials. In reality, the walker catches on everything and does its best to throw you violently to the ground. In addition, since you are supporting yourself on the walker, you are, by definition, already pressing down, thus systematically impeding any forward movement you have been able to muster. Your only defense is to pick up the walker with your hands, hurl it in front of you, hang on for dear life and drag yourself up behind it again. All this from a device that is supposed to keep you from falling down.

My walker comes with a little pull down seat that allows me to take a rest. Again, in theory, it is a good idea. To use it, however, you must pull it down, turn around and sit down over the little wheels. In my experience, when you sit on little wheels, they roll. As they start to roll, you must shift your weight forward (since you are sitting backwards) toward the back of the seat, so the little springs will allow the chair to stop rolling. And if you are not careful, you can expect to do a face plant out the back of the walker.

Now let us discuss the actual use of the walker at rest stops.

In Kentucky, we arrived at a brick roadside rest with beautiful curved sidewalks and lovely landscaping. As it was supposed to be, the handicapped parking was closest to the facilities. Unfortunately, there was still about a 150-yard walk uphill through the lovely landscaping. (I was tempted to park the van in the men's room.) I struggled up the hill, throwing the walker in front of me as I went. Forced to rest every 50 yards or so, I put down my little seat, turned around, and sat down over the little wheels. Immediately, I rolled backwards for several yards. Forward 50, backwards 20. Forward 50, backwards 20. I made the door in 20 minutes flat.

Exhausted, with sweat rolling down my face, I was faced with the difficult task of holding onto the walker, opening the door against its 600 pound return spring, and thrusting myself and the walker through the gap before the door slammed and crushed me like a large rat. After several attempts, a sympathetic truck driver took pity on me and held the door open. I then maneuvered myself and my instrument of torture through the next door into the men's room.

A man using a walker simply cannot walk up to a urinal. The walker with its little seat sits between you and the urinal and laughs. Therefore, you must now maneuver the walker around in back of you, still hanging on for dear life. Without going into great detail, you must continue to stand, maneuver your clothing, hit your target, all the while constantly holding on so that you do not fall. You could certainly use an extra set of hands, but truckers frown on your asking for help at a time like that. I considered using the little seat, but it would be embarrassing to be rolling backwards through the men's room.

I think in the future, I may take a roll of duct tape and duct tape myself to the plumbing. As you can see, being handicapped is not for sissies.

For a true baseball fan, this is the greatest time of year. I have been watching three or four baseball games a day for several weeks, first to see who got into the playoffs and now to see who advances. Yesterday I was bummed out when I had to leave Houston and Atlanta in the 11th inning in a 6-to-6 tie for my granddaughters' soccer game, even though I love to watch the girls play. When the soccer game was over, I was amazed to discover that the baseball game was in the 17th inning, and the Astros and Braves were still tied. I got to see Roger the Rocket win in 18 innings in his first relief appearance since the 1980s. It was the longest game in MLB post season history.

And just think; baseball will run for two more weeks! Beth is a saint.

Today is the two-year anniversary of my diagnosis. I am still alive, God is on his throne and I get to hang out with you folks a while longer. Life is good.

On Saturday, I had a flu shot and a pneumonia shot, which are essential for people like me. I had a common reaction to the pneumonia shot and was sick for two days. My breathing was worse than usual and I spent most of the weekend on my breathing machine. So what's new?

I have had several choking events, but none that required the emergency squad. We may have to deal with this on a regular basis. Now everyone in the family is afraid to leave me at home alone.

What Am I Learning? *"One Six Delta Charlie, you are cleared for the ILS approach, runway nine right. Please advise when you have the localizer."*

I had not been able to see out of the airplane since I took off and climbed into the "soup" two hours ago. The clouds and weather were so thick, it was as if somebody had painted over the windows. Everything was pitch black except the instrument panel. According to my Jeppesen charts, I was at the correct altitude, and on the proper heading. At this speed things happen fast and I had to be careful. I was looking for that little highway in the sky that would lead me safely to the runway. My instruments were on the right frequency.

The needle started to move and I turned toward the heading and called the tower. "Tower, One Six Delta Charlie, established on the localizer."

"Roger One Six Delta Charlie cleared to land runway nine right." I slowed the airplane and set everything for landing. As the glideslope needle centered, I started the airplane down. This little electronic pathway, called an ILS or Instrument Landing System, was supposed to lead me down through the clouds to a safe landing. The gear was down and locked; I had approach flaps and the fuel was on the proper tank. After what seemed like a long time, light began to filter up from below. Suddenly, at little more than 200 feet above actual ground level, I broke out of it. There in front of me, right where it was supposed to be and lit up like a Christmas tree, was about a mile of concrete calling me home. As my wheels squeaked down, I thanked God for another safe return.

An ILS is made up of two radio beams, one on a distinct compass heading in line with the runway and the other on a defined angle of descent designed to bring you down from altitude to the runway. It is the primary instrument landing system used at most larger airports. Daily, thousands of pilots worldwide put their faith in it to lead them through bad weather and land safely at their destinations. Most passengers do not even know it exists, though their lives depend on it. And in over 30 years of flying, I have never been able to see, touch or hear it, but ILS has always been there when I needed it.

An accomplished pilot, Dave enjoys the cockpit of this antique bird

I am posting this journal entry on October 28, 2005. It has been two full years to the day since the doctors told Beth and me that I have ALS and am going to die. My diagnosis has not changed. Though my life has been dramatically altered. I am still alive and in awe of all God has taught me.

While I have been sick, I have spent a lot of time thinking about faith. "Now faith is being sure of what we hope for, and certain of what we do not see." (Hebrews 11:1)

In over 43 years of walking with Jesus, I have never physically seen him, touched him or heard him, yet he has always been here when I need him. People ask me how I can be so sure about my future and where I am going. How do I know God is real and Jesus is really here for us? Faith. Just because we cannot experience Him with our senses does not mean he is not here, ready to guide us through this difficult life to our ultimate home with him. When we put our trust in him, we discover he keeps his promises. Over the last two years, he has shown me he is here, safer than any ILS.

Two years ago, I did not know anything about ALS or about the depth of suffering one could experience. I did not know anything of the magnitude of grief one could face as I slowly lost the use of one body part after another. I did not anticipate the loss I would feel in giving up the gym, golfing, biking, hiking and so many of the other activities I have loved. I did not understand the feelings of uselessness when I could not contribute in ways I always had. I did not understand the pain I would feel when I could not make my hands or legs work and I could not run after my grandchildren to play. I never understood how hard it would be to have my day revolve totally around medicine, vitamins, IVs, breathing machines and doctors. I knew nothing of wheelchairs, walkers, BiPAP machines, feeding tubes or nebulizers. I had never worried about falling down in public and not being able to get up. I never had to call the emergency squad because I could not breathe. I did not know what it was like to have what seemed like a garden hose shoved up my nose and down my throat. I had never gone to the hospital, had them tell me I had a heart attack, just to later tell me it was a mistake. I also never had to put everything in God's hands because before, I always thought I had my own resources. "If any man among you thinks himself one of the world's clever ones, let him discard his cleverness that he may learn to be truly wise. For this world's cleverness is stupidity to God." (1 Corinthians 3:18-19)

Since I am dying, I have no choice but to open my heart to let him work from within. As a result, I have learned a tremendous amount. He is teaching me the depth of his love, care, comfort, grace and joy in ways I could never have experienced otherwise. I have experienced his presence with me in the darkest nights when I was mired in despair. I have experienced the incredible depth of my friends' caring and prayers and love. I have been amazed to see the wonder of what God could do in a family as they suffer together and turn to him. I have watched God soften my heart to love and care for others as I never have before. I have witnessed God open opportunities before my very eyes for me to lift him up and help others see him. And he has comforted me and tenderly carried me where I could not go by myself.

Can we trust a God we cannot see? Two years ago, life was so blessedly abundant that it could be taken for granted. Days stretched out ahead of us, seemingly forever. Opportunities, possibilities, dreams and plans were there for the taking, and God was good. But it is two years later now. That endless time no longer spans out before us, assured and available. Life is so much harder than it was before. Spontaneity is gone. Every act becomes deliberate and every journey requires a battle plan and an entourage. Life is truly even more precious. Time is a treasured gift. Friendships have deepened and shed the superficial. Family life is an immeasurable blessing, holding an almost unimaginable sweetness. Blessings still rain down. God's touch feels more tender. Love is better somehow. And God is still good.

Does God really exist? Can we have faith in something that we cannot see, touch or feel? Absolutely. But we must set our instruments to receive his leading and we must watch for signs. We must read his Word and talk to him in prayer. He is here to lead us down that path through all the difficulties of life to an eternal home.

Beth and I want to thank you from the bottom of our hearts for the two years of prayer and caring. And here is an amazing fact. Not one day of those two years has gone by without tangibly experiencing your love, care, concern and prayers. What a testimony to the body of Christ as God intended it to function.

As Lou Gehrig said, "I'm the luckiest man in the world."

November 14, 2005

What Am I Learning? *As he shook hands with me, his hand seemed to engulf not only my hand, but my whole forearm…*

It was the biggest hand I had ever seen, yet it was so gentle. Donnie Brown and I were sitting alone in the general manager's box, as we so often did in that summer, watching the Pittsburgh Pirates play baseball, when his father hurried in. "Come with me quickly, boys. I want you to meet somebody." I had no idea who we were going to meet, but from the expression on Mr. Brown's face, it had to be somebody important.

Mr. Brown ushered us into the owner's box, pretty heady territory for a 15-year-old. The next thing I knew, I was shaking hands with Joe Louis. Winner of 69 professional boxing bouts, 55 by knockout, the former heavyweight champion affectionately known as the "Brown Bomber" was arguably the greatest fighter who ever lived. A boxing fan for many years, I knew everything about Joe Louis. In 1938, with the United States inching toward war with Germany, it was Louis, a black American, who fought Max Schmeling of Germany. It is hard to understand today how terribly important this fight was between a representative of Nazi Germany's "master race" and this black man, born poor in a log cabin. When he knocked Schmeling to the canvas in the first round, his win was for a nation and the world. And there I was, staring up at this gentle giant. Louis had been retired for 11 years, but when you looked at his hand, you could see it was powerful enough to crush a man's cheekbones. Despite his many accomplishments, he spent the next hour quietly talking to me about my world, not his. All the glamour and his many accomplishments mattered not to him; he gave his full attention to a 15-year-old kid.

All my life I have dreamed of doing big things like Joe Louis. Today I tried to make coffee. My hands would not work. I spilled the water and, after I ground the beans, I knocked the coffeemaker apart and spilled the grounds all over the counter and the floor. With a wet rag, I was only successful in smearing the mess across the kitchen and I had to wait until Beth got home to vacuum the floor. After a full 30 minutes of tiring labor, angry and frustrated, I finally got a cup of coffee.

Through it all, God is teaching me a tremendous lesson. I am learning there is joy in being where he wants me, even if it is a very lowly position.

Mechanics just left my house, and I have a new electric stair lift. Now in addition to wheelchair races, I can offer my grandkids rides up and down the stairs.

What Am I Learning? *This Thursday is Thanksgiving. Traditionally, it is a time for families to gather together, overeat, watch football and thank God for all the blessings he has bestowed upon them. It is my favorite holiday. While it may involve endless dishwashing, it also involves endless eating and a huge overdose of football and family laughs. Unfortunately, for many, the giving thanks part rarely takes the forefront.*

Over the years, when I have contemplated those things for which I am thankful, I am often appalled by the shallowness of my response. I'm approaching Thanksgiving from a completely different perspective this year.

As I have watched my body slowly dying, I have also watched my spirit slowly awakening. I am learning that, while I cannot breathe easily, I can thank God that I can breathe. While I can no longer walk, I can thank God that I can stand. While I can no longer run, my grandchildren love wheelchair racing. We can learn to thank God in our suffering.

A Different Kind of Hero: Me and My Papa
by Claire Chilcoat, age 7
"My Papa is my hero because he is sick
but he still tells jokes and cheers people up."
National PTA 2004/05 Reflection Program
Ohio Winner

CHAPTER 9

Winter

Daunting Circumstances and Dearest Gifts

December 1, 2005

For the first time, our house is decorated for Christmas and I had nothing to do with it. While Beth and granddaughter Abby decorated the house, I took a nap. Amazingly it was not nearly as tiring this year.

It has become increasingly difficult to get me out of the house. We have to take so much equipment with us and fit it between breathing treatments. But there is always a silver lining. Because it is hard to get out and since I do not drive anymore, friends bring lunch to the house if they want to see me. This way, I do not have to buy lunch and if you know most of my friends, this is the only way they would ever spring for the check.

December 19, 2005

I am finally getting my new wheelchair, custom-built for me. It's bright red and is much faster than my old one. The name of the manufacturer is on it, but I think it is really a Ferrari.

The day after Christmas, we had a family reunion with my brothers' families. We had a great time with all the little grandkids running around, playing games and looking at old pictures. I did wheelchair racing with the grandkids, but I must be careful with my new chair since it is so fast. On its highest settings, I can actually pull a wheelie.

I have lost so much muscle I am concerned about pressure sores. We are experimenting with different kinds of cushions for my wheelchair. I only sleep on my sides in bed since that is the only way I can breathe, even with my breathing machine, but my hipbones get so sore that the pain wakes me up. I hope the doctors can give us some ideas for relief.

Dave was cowboy hero Hopalong Cassidy

What Am I Learning? *When I was four years old, I was Hopalong Cassidy. I wore my favorite Hopalong Cassidy shirt* *every day. I carried duel silver pistols, and rode my imaginary horse, Topper. By the time I was six, I had graduated to Sky King. It was amazing how many bad guys I could thwart as I flew my twin-engine Cessna everywhere. I dabbled as the Lone Ranger and Captain Midnight for a while, but in seventh grade I became James Bond, 007. Not only did I carry a Beretta automatic pistol, but I was also old enough to appreciate the Bond women. In early high school, I fancied myself as the next Joe Bellino, the Naval Academy's running back known affectionately as the "Pocket Battleship." At 5'9" and 181 pounds, Bellino won the 1960 Heisman Trophy. I was 5'9", so why shouldn't I be as famous as Joe Bellino? In each of the imaginary roles I chose to play, I was always a hero.*

Beth and I want our Savior to be the hero who will vanquish evil right now and right all the wrongs immediately, especially the wrongs that affect us. We want a hero who will meet our every need. We want a hero with big guns. We sat up in bed last night, talking into the early morning. We prayed and we cried.

We were talking about my death.

It was a hard conversation. She is my best friend, and I do not want her to be alone. I need a hero. My physical condition is real, and I need a hero who has real answers even in the face of death. I need a hero who can provide comfort and peace and joy despite my deteriorating physical condition. I need a hero who can take care of Beth and my loved ones, even when I cannot.

In this life, we do not get to ride off into the sunset with all problems solved and foes vanquished. But Jesus points us to the God who loves us so much he died for us. So Jesus is my hero. I can trust him with life's daunting circumstances and life's dearest gifts. And I do not have to fear death because it is not the end.

"For where now, O death, is your power to hurt us? Where now, O grave, is the victory you hope to win? It is sin, which gives death its sting, and it is the Law, which gives sin its strength. All thanks to God, then, who gives us the victory over these things through our Lord Jesus Christ!" (1 Corinthians 15:55-57)

January 5, 2006

I have increased cramping in my arms and hands. The disease is now moving on since there is little left of my legs.

Fortunately, I am still doing well enough to spend a lot of time with my grandkids. We continue our family tradition of winter campouts in front of the fireplace in our family room. This is something we did for years with our own children and have continued with their families. We get out the sleeping bags, cook dinner over the fire and tell silly ghost stories. I do not think I will sleep on the floor this year. My machinery might keep everybody awake. At least that is the excuse I am using. Age has its privileges.

January 23, 2006

Though it was a tough trip down, we're back in Florida enjoying the weather. With my new high-speed wheelchair and Beth's bicycle, we took the bike trail from my mother-in-law's house to downtown Clearwater and back, covering about 12 miles. We had a wonderful time. Beth thought it was great exercise, but I did not feel tired at all. I must be in better shape than I thought, although some skeptics will say it is because I have a motor on the wheelchair.

February 1, 2006

Our trip to Florida by car was difficult enough that I thought we had made a major mistake by coming. As friends and family heard about it, an amazing thing happened. We received offer after offer from people willing to fly here and drive us back, or drive down and caravan back with us. Thank you for your kind thoughts and generous proposals. What a demonstration of God's love.

February 9, 2006

Two weeks ago Sherpa Beth (also known as Captain Beth) and the Terribly Handicapped Traveler (also known as the Backseat Driver or the Director of Advice) headed south to Florida. In this week's episode, our hero and heroine attempt the return trip to Columbus, Ohio, armed only with tenacity, steel wills, sincere faith and an invaluable air cushion for the Director of Advice's rear end.

As the curtain opens, it is Thursday morning in Clearwater, Florida, and Sherpa Beth is loading the wheelchair van. During the night, she has packed all nonessential items, including her disassembled bicycle, the manual wheelchair, the walker, the nonessential medical bag, both portable nebulizers, all hanging clothes, all clothing not required to be worn on the trip home, three boxes of fresh grapefruits and oranges, the briefcase and computer and all other items not needed during the night or in the morning, so that the morning departure can be hastened. Having analyzed all aspects of the return trip and repacked all essential medicines, travel clothes and toiletries into a single bag, Sherpa Beth, as driver, is anticipating a much easier return voyage. Both of our characters have bathed the return trip in prayer and are anticipating God's deliverance. The Director of Advice will be riding in the back in his wheelchair giving true credence to his new title, "The Backseat Driver."

Arising early in anticipation of departure, Sherpa Beth showers, dresses, eats breakfast, walks the dog and then waits patiently for the Director of Advice to wake so they may depart at the crack of 11:00 a.m. Sherpa Beth assists her husband into the shower, helps him shave and brush his teeth, dresses him, feeds him, helps him nebulize, helps him vibrate his chest, secures his power wheelchair in the van with him in it, loads the dog, loads the nebulizer, loads the chest vibration machine, loads the breathing machine, kisses her mother goodbye and drives out of the driveway at 10:41 a.m. They are on record pace!

Unable to do the driving for the first time in their 36-year marriage, the Director of Advice is less than cute, according to Captain Beth, barking key instructions: "Go north. Slow down. Watch out." Sherpa Beth pays no heed, other than to his occasional reading of road signs due to her inability to see beyond the end of her nose, even with her glasses. Speeding north a full 20 miles since departure, everything appears to be going well. Suddenly, the speedometer quits working. Having seen this before, the Backseat Driver calmly informs Captain Beth not to worry. "We have probably broken our speedometer cable. We will just keep up with traffic. It should not delay us getting home." Within a matter of minutes however, the speedometer leaps from zero to 120 miles an hour and the transmission tries to shift down. This unfortunate behavior begins to occur every few minutes with frightening regularity. The Backseat Driver now changes his assessment to, "Houston, we have a problem."

Our intrepid travelers call a Dodge dealership, 80 miles north, and are connected with the service manager who says, "Nobody uses speedometer cables anymore. It all runs by computer. You are obviously having a computer problem," which is very reassuring to our couple, since they still have 75 miles to go. As they buck their way north, the Director of Advice keeps up a constant fusillade of meaningful advice. "Back off the gas. Accelerate slowly. Do not pass. Keep going north." All of this is merrily received by Captain Beth.

At the Dodge dealer, our intrepid travelers are advised that for a mere $525, they can be back on the road in three hours. In keeping with their normal response to trouble, the Terribly Handicapped Traveler sits at the car dealership with the dog in order to be able to offer invaluable advice to the mechanics, while Sherpa Beth goes shopping.

Once the repairs are made, they attempt to raise the van's wheelchair ramp, but it will only go up about a foot. It takes 10 minutes to discover that a piece of luggage has fallen against one of the switches giving it a command to go down, while the other switch commands it to go up. Electronically this does not work. A readjustment of the luggage cures the problem.

At four o'clock they depart once more with constant good humor. They had not planned to travel at night but that seems to be their only option. Having bathed the return trip in prayer, they cannot see how anything else can go wrong. They are oh, so mistaken!

As darkness falls, the skies open up and a torrential rain

envelopes them, rain so heavy they are slowed to a crawl. (Later they learn that eight inches fell along their route within a few hours.) As trucks pass them, visibility is near zero. Captain Beth is overcome with gratitude for the continuing stream of good advice she receives from the backseat. For his part, the Terribly Handicapped Traveler is enjoying the fact that the status of his rear end escalated from painful to excruciating somewhere around Valdosta, Georgia.

Finally arriving at their hotel stop, they pull into the handicapped space in front of their room. Unbeknownst to either traveler, there is a piece of broken metal sticking out from the curb which rips through the plastic bumper, tearing a hole up toward the grill. The Director of Advice is quick to point out that the damage probably will not exceed $2,000.

Since it is still raining, the Terribly Handicapped Traveler hurriedly backs his wheelchair up to exit the van. Meanwhile a tie-down strap stealthily loops around the left motor engagement switch of the wheelchair quietly turning it off. Now resting halfway in the van and halfway out on the ramp in the rain, the Terribly Handicapped Traveler finds himself unable to move or understand why only half of the wheelchair is working. Finally discovering the loop of cloth wrapped around the motor controller, he laughs merrily, encouraging our smiling Sherpa Beth to muscle the wheelchair back into the van far enough to disengage the loop and reengage the motor controller. This subjects Sherpa Beth to the same wonderfully refreshing rain shower the Director of Advice is enjoying. At long last they settle in their motel room, reflecting on how smoothly the day has gone and on the ample evidence of God answering their prayers for an easy travel day.

What Am I Learning? *I have obviously been poking fun, but every event I mentioned really did happen. Beth and I had prayed for our return trip, as had so many of you.*

If God is for us and we have asked him to ease our travels, why did we have such a difficult day? Interestingly enough, we did not pray any differently for the second day of our trip and yet it was easy, sunny and trouble free. Why is that?

Looking back, Beth and I can actually see many answers to prayers that first day: we made it to the Dodge dealer; the service manager was extremely kind and helpful – and was actually able to fix the car; the car did not break down at night when everything was closed or in the mountains far from help; the troubles with the van ramp and wheelchair motor were only temporary; the damage to the bumper did not strand us; and as we attempted to rest in God's love, we felt his presence with us throughout the day. It was simply a matter of our looking to him.

Beth and I often find ourselves saying something like, "God is so good because we had an easy trip," or "God is so good, because the children are healthy." We identify God's goodness with the result for which we are praying. But God is good even when our trip is not easy or when our health has failed. As you can imagine, Beth and I prayed much more fervently when we were having car trouble and were much more grateful for God's hand in our lives as he walked us through the struggles of that difficult travel day.

God knows real joy comes through our faith in him and not in the circumstances. His goodness does not hinge upon whether or not I have an easy life, or even if I am healed of ALS, nor does it depend on whether I suffer. His goodness is evidenced by his power and comfort in every situation, in his assured grace-filled promise of heaven and in his gracious provision for getting me there.

"Now to him who is able to keep you from falling and to present you before his glory without fault and with unspeakable joy, to the only God, our Savior, be glory and Majesty, power and authority, through Jesus Christ our Lord, before time was, now, and in all ages to come, Amen." (Jude 24-25)

The week started well: our daughter Jenny released her first CD of original praise music. Some of the music she wrote comes directly out of our struggle with ALS.[3]

However, our joy turned to sadness when my beloved mother suffered a massive stroke on Sunday. The doctors have told us she will not survive. As we sit in the hospital beside this little crusader for Christ waiting for Jesus to take her home, we are excited for her even though our hearts are breaking for our loss.

What Am I Learning? *My dear mother died this week. She just quit breathing early in the morning last Monday. The nurses said it was quiet, but of course they could not hear the angels singing and the huge party going on in Heaven. Mom was coming home.*

"You must not let yourselves be distressed – you must hold on to your faith in God and to your faith in me. There are many rooms in my Father's house. If there were not, should I have told you that I'm going away to prepare a place for you? It is true that I am going away to prepare a place for you, but it is just as true that I'm coming again to welcome you into my own home, so that you may be where I am." (John 14:1-3)

I do not know what Mom's room looks like in God's mansion. But I do know that Mom is there and she is happy. I know that there is a room waiting for me also, because God has promised there will be. What a comfort to know what lies on the other side.

It was difficult to watch Mom lying in bed at the hospital unable to move or speak. Now we know her suffering is over and she is in a perfect place.

"He who sits upon the throne will be their shelter. They will never again know hunger or thirst. The sun shall never beat upon

---

[3] See page 139 to read the lyrics of *Godspeed*, a song Jenny wrote for her dad.

them, neither shall there be any scorching heat, for the Lamb who is in the center of the throne will be their shepherd and will lead them to springs of living water. And God will wipe away every tear from their eyes." (Revelation 7:16-17)

Mom is home and, for her, there is no more pain or suffering. She is free.

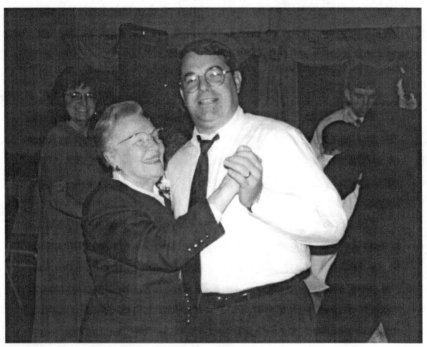

Dave and his mother Mildred Chilcoat

CHAPTER 10

Spring
Hope Stronger than My Distress

March 5, 2006

My BiPAP broke on Monday and I could not get a new one until 1:30 a.m. Amazingly, the new one broke 11.8 hours later. They delivered a second new one at 6:00 p.m. on Tuesday. When I went up to bed Tuesday night, the newest BiPAP would not work at all, and I did not get another one that worked until 2:30 a.m. The home health-care company said they had never seen anything like it. As a result, I did not sleep much for several days.

I am getting a new hospital bed and a new low-air-loss mattress, which should help my soreness. I am also getting a neck brace on Tuesday and braces for my hands, so they will not curl as much at night.

What Am I Learning? *For 21 years I have met every Monday morning with two Christian brothers. We share what is going on in our lives, hold one another accountable to God's Word and pray together. For ten years I have met every Wednesday morning with a group of eight men to study, share and pray. These are men who share a common, strong faith in Jesus Christ and a real love for each other. The friendships are deep. For years, both meetings* *took place at my office. When I got too sick to go to the office, both groups moved the meetings to my house so I could show up in my sweats without showering or shaving.*

This last Monday I sadly told my friends it was no longer possible for me to get up, get my braces and pants on and get downstairs by eight o'clock. They immediately proposed we move our meeting to lunch at my house on Mondays. The Wednesday group also moved to lunches instead of mornings. I had suggested that I should drop out of both, but no one would consider it.

The study group surrounds Dave in his sunroom (L to R): Nathan Shaw, Tim Heintzelman, D.G. Edgerton, Rob Crocker, Jeff Chilcoat, Ed Chilcoat and Greg Ball

It means so much to me that my friends are willing to change their schedules and disrupt their days so we can continue to share our lives. I get emotional when I realize the depth of our love for each other. Over the years, God has permitted Beth and me to develop a number of deep, sincere relationships with others from which we draw real joy and strength. It was the attractiveness of relationships like these that caused me to consider Christianity in the first place.

While it is true that we must make our individual decision to ask Jesus into our lives as our Lord and Savior, it is also true that God calls us to be part of the fellowship of believers. The love of an entire group of believers can leave a powerful impact.

What Am I Learning? *"Be merciful to me, O Lord, for I am in distress; my eyes grow weak with sorrow, my soul and my body with grief. My life is consumed by anguish and my years by groaning; my strength fails because of my affliction, and my bones grow weak." (Psalm 31:9-10)*

My new medical mattress arrived today. I was very excited to feel the relief. My brother Ed put it together. We turned on the computer controller. It inflated and deflated air tubes within the mattress that were designed to turn me from side to side. But as I lay on it, I realized I was not going to get any relief. It could not turn me enough. After a few minutes my backside was on fire again. To make matters worse, I could not move at all in the bed. When I tried to push with my hands to move myself, I was push-ing on air. That realization was crushing. I was going to continue to be in pain.

The disappointment and discouragement were so palpable all I could do was cry. I have lost 50 pounds of muscle and have no pad-ding over my bones, so I'm in great pain when sitting. Everything on me aches, and pain is more difficult when there is no anticipation of relief.

"In you, O Lord, I have taken refuge; let me never be put to shame; deliver me in your righteousness. Turn your ear to me, come quickly to my rescue; be my rock of refuge, a strong fortress to save me." (Psalm 31:1-2)

In Matthew 14:22-32, we read the story of Jesus walking on the water toward his disciples. It was a stormy night and the wind and waves were directly against their boat. When they saw him they were terribly frightened. Peter said to Jesus, "Lord, if it's really you, tell me to come to you on the water." Jesus tells him to come. Peter actually walked on the water toward Jesus.

Peter had enough faith in Jesus to get out of the boat and begin to walk. But when he saw all the trouble around him, he was frightened and he panicked. He took his eyes off Jesus and focused on the waves. As he did so, his own strength failed him and he began to go down.

I am no different.

I want to believe in Jesus, that he will take care of everything. But when I see the trouble around me, I panic.

I desperately want to be God's man. But I am like Peter. When my suffering gets heavy and my pain is intense, I find it easy to forget God. I panic. I do not know why I have this disease. I do not know why every day it gets worse. I do not know why the mattress did not work.

Today I am Peter, struggling to keep my eyes on God instead of on the waves and the fury of the wind. Today I am Peter, afraid the water will overcome me.

Lord, by your hand and through the power of your Holy Spirit, let me stay the course. Though my feet are wet, I will continue to look to you, Jesus, to see what mighty works you will perform.

March 24, 2006

Sunday morning I had the amazing opportunity to baptize our ninth grandchild, Owen Andrew Chilcoat. It was wonderful.

The ALS Association loaned us a gel foam pad to put over my hospital bed mattress. It seems to help some with my soreness. In addition, we bought a heavy-duty cargo net of sewn nylon strapping, the kind made for pickup truck beds. By gripping the webbing, I can raise myself to a sitting position. This allows me much more freedom of movement in bed. We had to order it, so Beth made a temporary one of nylon rope for me to use until our mail-order one arrived. Who would guess that my sweet bride has the skill to make a stevedore's cargo net?

We also got window coverings for the sunroom where I am sleeping. For the last two weeks, I have been mooning my neighbors. I think they will be very grateful for the shades.

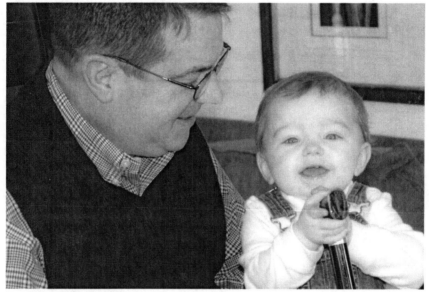

Owen on his Papa's lap

April 1, 2006

I have not felt good lately, but it is Saturday and there is PGA golf, the Final Four, Pirates baseball and Blue Jackets hockey on TV. Beth is really looking forward to the day so she can watch all of it with me.

If you believe that, I got you. It's April Fools' Day!

Despite feeling crummy, Beth and I were able to get out to a park to walk (and wheel chair) around a lake for an hour when the temperature got up to 70. It was wonderful.

What Am I Learning? *"For this reason a man will leave his father and mother and be united to his wife, and the two will become one flesh." (Ephesians 5:31)*

She helps me out of my wheelchair and onto my hospital bed.

117

She lifts my legs up onto the bed and pushes me across the bed to the far side. She adjusts my breathing mask and makes sure I am comfortable. Then she lifts the hose of my breathing machine over her head and lies down beside me. We hold each other tight and pray. After a while, she kisses me good night and goes up to our old bedroom. It is not your typical bedroom scene from the movies, but this is a real marriage. It was not always this way.

Beth and I met in college at the University of Pittsburgh where we were both working with Young Life. We became really good friends. In those days the Pirates played at Forbes Field, which was just across the street from our dorms. We would study until about eight o'clock, get a quick, cheap dinner at the Original Hot Dog stand and walk to Forbes Field. During the seventh inning, they let us sit in the bleachers for free. Since Beth and I had very little money, we watched a lot of two inning games. Those were wonderful days. We were part of a huge fellowship of Christians involved with Young Life and we were learning to love each other and God. I knew right away I wanted to marry this girl, but I had to ask her at least 200 times before she finally said yes.

When we got married in 1969, we were the first of our group of college friends to do so. We were young and stupid and did not know much about being married. When I was growing up, my dad's job was to go to the office and work. When he came home he did not have to do anything. Beth's dad, on the other hand, was involved in every aspect of household and family life. I was perfectly happy to let Beth do the housework, but I slowly perceived as I sat and watched TV every evening, that she might have a different perspective. On the other hand, whatever would possess a woman to want to go for a walk and talk when the Steelers were about to kick off on the television? Slowly the light began to dawn on both of us that there were things we could do for the other, even if they were not what we were used to. God began to teach us.

We have become even better able to let go of self and love each other. This has been evident as I have watched my beautiful bride respond to my illness. For years Beth and I walked together in the evenings so we could talk. She walked faster than me and I had to push myself to keep up. But as I slowed down because of the illness, she slowed down also, without saying a word. As my hands started giving me trouble, she started opening bottles for me and cutting my food. She took over fastening my buttons, pulling up my pants and putting on my shoes and socks. When my fingers could no longer manipulate and sort my pills or write notes, Beth did it. I could no longer clean my glasses, so Beth did. Whatever I needed she has done, no matter how menial. She never complains. She is not my right hand; she and I have become one flesh. We are one.

Best friends and God's gifts to each other

Since I have been sick, I have spent a lot of time looking at my partner. Even though our vows said, "...in sickness and in health," it is hard to imagine how difficult this situation has become for Beth. (I met a man a couple years ago who also had ALS. He told me that shortly after his diagnosis his wife left him. As she walked out the door, she told him, "I did not sign up for this.") Our marriage is not perfect, but it is centered in Christ. As we submit to Christ, we learn how to submit to each other and the marriage works. Christ-centeredness has given us the strength to continue to function when our world seems to be crashing down on us.

Beth and I used to ski. We used to hike in the woods and climb mountains. We are not able to do that anymore. But we love each other with a passion that is beyond words. God has given us an amazing gift. It may not play well in Hollywood, but it plays well in our home.

April 10, 2006

Since I sit so much, as the day goes along my feet swell. My doctor says I am highly susceptible to blood clots. He has prescribed compression hose, which should help ease the swelling in my legs and feet. And, of course, they are really attractive.

What Am I Learning? *Each morning, I do not get out of bed until God and I have spoken and I have given him back the day which he has been so kind to give me. If I am going to suffer, I do not want any of it to be wasted.*

April 27, 2006

What Am I Learning? *I had been running. I had actually been running at full speed over a grass-covered field. It was awesome to have the wind in my face again, to be able to make my legs stretch out and cover the ground so fast. Pick them up and put them down. It was effortless. What an incredible feeling of freedom! What a letdown when I realized I was still in bed. It had been a dream.*

Actually, I had been anticipating this dream for a long time. How could I not dream about being able to walk and run again? Yet it had taken two years to have the dream. As I lay there in bed, I thought about how good it would be to be normal again.

My Pirates lost again last night. That makes us 8 wins and 23 losses. I used to think I was finished playing all sports since I cannot walk or stand up, my hands do not work, I cannot breathe and my arms are weak. However, after watching the Pirates closely, I think I might be able not only to play for them, but to actually star.

What Am I Learning? *Hospice came this week. It was surreal, sitting there calmly talking about making my death easier and how to ease my breathing so I will not feel like I am choking. It was hard on Beth.*

Neither of us can imagine this is really happening. It is not like planning for other future events. But it is what it is. And God knows. In fact he is the only one who knows the number of my days. He could still heal me; he certainly has the power.

The hospice nurse explained that many people think of hospice only in terms of death and dying. Hospice is about making the life you have left comfortable and enjoyable. Hospice also develops a plan for dealing with death. There is a real parallel between that aspect of hospice and the Christian faith. Hospice is about equipping us to die. Christianity is also about equipping us to die. We can die without hospice, but it may not be a comfortable death. We can also die without Christ. That definitely will not be a comfortable death. When we die without Christ, we do not live for eternity with God.

Just like the hospice patient, we are all dying. God's hospice is available to us all. We only have to ask.

Beth called me to dinner at seven o'clock the other night. The Pirates were on TV with the first pitch at 7:05. I figured I would only miss the top of the first inning. When I returned to the TV at 7:15, it was already Florida 5, Pittsburgh 0 and we were only in the bottom of the first. I do not think the World Series is in our future this fall.

I am having more bad days than good. Hospice is actively involved now. They immediately got me a new mattress, which should lessen my soreness. They also provided a suction machine, which helps if I start to choke and is probably better than my shop vac. They have taken over my medications, which should save us quite a bit of money. They are giving me a new pain medication, which helps my aching. However, it makes me sleepy, so I take it only at bedtime. They also have given me a little pill that fools my body into thinking I am breathing better than I am. It does not improve my breathing, but my brain does not know it. And some of you thought I was actually smart!

What Am I Learning? *I awoke at 2:45 this morning and rolled onto my back. Since I cannot breathe for long on my back, I raised the head of the hospital bed to 30°. I then reached with my left hand to find the edge of the cargo net. I straightened the fingers on my right hand, so I could grip it. Grasping the net with both hands, I tried to pull myself up into a sitting position. I did not have enough strength to do it. Letting go with my right hand, I pushed my right leg over the side of the bed to make the pull easier. Even so, I could not get up. Letting go again I pushed my left leg to the side of the bed. Pulling again on the cargo net with all my might, I managed to get up onto my left elbow, but I could go no further. I was now stretched sideways across the bed with my legs hanging over the side and my back flat on the bed, like a turtle lying on the back of its shell. I could not move. Breathing was extremely difficult in this position, even with my BiPAP. I needed to do something quickly, before I ran out of air. I groped with my right hand for the cell phone attached to the string on the side of my bed. When I was able to retrieve it, I pressed the speed dial to call Beth. She came running and got me up.*

I know at some point it will be necessary for us to get help during the night, but I so want to resist that until it is absolutely necessary. I hate the idea of being a burden. Also it is humiliating to have a stranger dress me or assist me when I need help to relieve myself. How do I maintain my dignity?

This is a lousy way to live, Lord. Yet you are God and I am not. I know you are here with me even in the darkest hour. I know it by the tender mercies and loving promises you whisper to me in the still of the night. Your beauty outside my window wakes me in the morning and your stillness and peace put me to bed at night. Even now, Lord, with these weak arms and tears in my eyes, I lift my hands and praise you. How precious it is that you care for me through each moment of my sorrow.

"He will wipe every tear from their eyes. There will be no more death or mourning or crying or pain, for the old order of things has passed away." (Revelation 21:4)

I praise you, God, for loving me. Thank you for wiping away the tears and giving me hope and a future with you. Thank you for a hope that is stronger than my distress.

CHAPTER 11

Summer
I Am Free!

June 1, 2006

As difficult as this last week has been, absolute miracles do happen: the Pirates scored 36 runs and actually swept the Milwaukee Brewers four straight games!

What Am I Learning? *My eyes popped open at three in the morning. It was the beginning of several very difficult days. The pain in my back was excruciating, but I could not move to relieve the pressure. As the muscles of my chest wall and rib cage have weakened, my ribs are collapsing on top of one another and I am getting a lot of pain across my back, under my shoulder blades. If I do not sit bolt upright, I can feel my ribs rubbing against each other. It makes breathing difficult and it makes me very tired. I have a high pain threshold, but this is just too much. All Beth and I could do was get me out of bed, give me a breathing treatment and take more pain medicine.*

At the ALS clinic, the doctors were blunt. When my breathing gets down to about 20%, the CO_2 buildup will be too much and I will die. I will simply go to sleep and not wake up. In the meantime, they will try to control my pain with medication. None of *the doctors would venture a guess as to how long that progression would take.*

Beth and I have been praying about using a respirator and it does not seem it is the way to go. The disease will continue to progress regardless of the respirator. It is a difficult choice everyone with ALS must make. Beth and I pray every night that God will intervene and let us grow old together. It is extremely hard on both of us. How do you say goodbye to your best friend?

June 11, 2006

I continue to see significant physical deterioration. I quickly hit a wall and find myself in serious pain and not able to breathe. Transferring out of my wheelchair has become a problem, with falls several times this week. Fortunately I have strong sons who can muscle me back up. I now only transfer if I have somebody on both sides of me.

Hospice provided me with a more comfortable bed. Even so, I need someone to turn me every two hours, since I cannot move in bed. So far it seems to be working fairly well with family members taking turns.

What Am I Learning? *My brother Ed recently sent me a great Far Side® cartoon. The first scene, entitled "The Names We Give Dogs," shows two men talking. The first man tells his friend, "This is Rex, our new dog." The second scene, entitled "The Names They Give Themselves," shows Rex introducing himself to two other dogs: "Hello, I am known as Vexorg, Destroyer of Cats and Devourer of Chickens." The other two dogs respond, "I am Zornorph, The One Who Comes by Night to the Neighbor's Yard, and this is Princess Shewana, Barker of Great Annoyance and Daughter of Queen La Stainer of Persian Rugs."*

Often we refer to ourselves as Christians, yet for many in this modern world the name Christian is negative, someone who is arrogant, prejudiced, judgmental and two-faced. The term is often interchangeable with European Western culture and has little to do with Jesus. This meaning of the name Christian is not one to which I aspire. I want to be known as "a man of God."

What name would you like God to call you? When you get to heaven's gate and Jesus reaches out to welcome you home to live with him, by what greeting will you be welcomed? Perhaps you think he will call you Sinner, but instead he calls you Forgiven. Perhaps you call yourself Brokenhearted, but he will call you Comforted. You may expect him to greet you as Failure, but your name will be Victorious. You answer to Ugly and Ashamed, but Jesus calls you Beautiful and Restored. You may feel Guilty and Condemned, but he sees you by your real names, Redeemed and Freed.

God is calling us by our new names, names such as Dearly Beloved, Child of God and Redeemed of the World. If we are willing to trust that in his Son we are freely forgiven and now reflect the very image of Christ, we can be instruments for his purposes. We can truly find joy, both now and for eternity in heaven with him. We can be used by God to teach others to know the forgiveness and peace of life in Christ.

By what name do I want Jesus to greet me at the gates of heaven? I am looking forward to Jesus reaching out his hand to welcome me and calling me his "Good and Faithful Servant." I can think of nothing more thrilling!

June 20, 2006

What Am I Learning? *When he was little, every evening I would pick him up and gently lay him on my bed on a stack of pillows. I would lie down beside him and read his favorite story,* Poppa Geezer and the Bogeyman. *Next we prayed together. Then I carried him to his room, kissed him goodnight and put him in his bed. It was the ritual that my youngest son Andy and I went through every night to get him to sleep.*

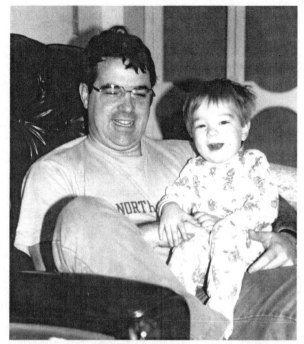

**Dave lovingly cared for baby Andy; in time, Andy did
the same for his dad**

*Our ritual has changed now. When he hears me call him on the
baby monitor, he comes to my room. He gives me a drink of water,
empties my urinal and gives me my medication. Then he gently lifts
my emaciated body and places me on the other side of the bed. He
tenderly rolls me on my side, places a pillow between my legs and a
pillow in front of me and covers me up. He kisses me good night. I
am in a new position to sleep for another hour and a half, until the
pain wakes me. He is there through the night, listening, ready to get
up and help me just like I was with him years ago. Oh how life has
changed! The next night it will be Jeff, then Michael, then Nathan.
The love of a family comes straight from God.*

*There is no question in my mind that I am dying. For the last
three weeks I have spent most of my time on my breathing machine,
in and out of wakefulness between doses of morphine for pain. I love
my family more than anyone can imagine, but there are times when
death does not seem a bad choice.*

My Pirates just set a new record. Unfortunately it was for the longest losing streak in team history. Last night they successfully lost their 13th straight. And I never thought they would be good at anything!

The Old Testament speaks of David's Mighty Men, those warriors who served King David. A number of men from our church, Faith Covenant, have volunteered to lose sleep along with family members and other friends, just to turn me in bed each night. Beth has taken to calling them "David's Merciful Men." God is teaching me to humbly accept the loving gifts of others.

As my health degenerates, I find it more and more difficult to keep up my writing, but I hope to continue. I am so honored to be able to write this journal each week.

What Am I Learning? *The sun is shining on my backyard this morning. The sky is a deep blue and a light wind is blowing the leaves of the trees. There are many colorful flowers in the beds outside my windows. It is beautiful! You are here with me, Lord. You sit beside me, and we enjoy the beauty of your creation together. Thank you, Lord. Life has been so difficult lately. You know my struggle to breathe. Even after the doctors changed the settings on my breathing machine, getting enough air is a struggle. My pain is constant without the morphine, but when I get enough morphine to break through the pain, I cannot stay awake. You are all I have, Lord, my refuge and my strength.*

"Answer me when I call to you, O my righteous God. Give me relief from my distress; be merciful to me and hear my prayer. I will lie down and sleep in peace, for you alone, O Lord, make me dwell in safety." (Psalm 4:1,8)

Today is Beth's birthday. We are going to have a quiet family celebration here at home. Next to Jesus, she is the best thing that ever happened to me.

What Am I Learning? *I knew I was in trouble the minute they laid me down in bed. No matter what position I took, I could not breathe. I had my allotted dosage of morphine and I still hurt. I prayed that God would calm my insides so my breathing would relax. I asked Beth and Andy to lift me back into my wheelchair. Although I had just nebulized, we did it again. Nothing brought relief. I told Beth to call the Hospice emergency number. Beth asked me what to say if they recommended putting me in Kobacker House, their special hospital. I told her to have them put me in. That scared her, because it is where you go to die.*

As it turned out, the hospice nurse was able to talk us through medication changes allowing me to sleep without going to Kobacker. Unfortunately, we are struggling with the same issues each night. The hospice people talk to us in terms of days or weeks.

I am getting worse. My pain is increasing and I spend most of my day sleeping. It is almost impossible to accomplish anything. Writing is very difficult. I have a hard time reading, even the Bible. I start to read and then realize I have fallen asleep.

I am not afraid. My God is with me and he comforts me. "Never will I leave you, never will I forsake you." (Hebrews 13:5b) My primary sadness and anxiety centers in my love and concern for my family and friends. It is almost unbearable to think of not being with them. I have a difficult time turning them over to God. Even at this point in my journey, I fail to be the man who trusts God with everything. Thanks be to God for his amazing grace that overcomes this lack of trust. I know he cares about them and loves them even more than I do.

I do not know when or if I will be able to write again, but there is one thing I do not want to leave this life without expressing to you. "We are writing to you about something which has always existed, yet which we ourselves actually saw and heard: something which we had opportunity to observe closely and even to hold in our hands, and yet, as we know now, was something of the very Word of life himself! For it was life *which appeared before us: we saw it, we are eyewitnesses of it, and are now writing to you about it. It was the very life of all ages, the life that has always existed with the Father, which actually became visible in person to us mortal men. We repeat, we really saw and heard what we are now writing to you about. We want you to be with us in this – in this fellowship with the Father, and Jesus Christ his Son. We must write and tell you about it, because the more that fellowship extends, the greater the joy it brings to us who are already in it. Here, then, is the message which we heard from him, and now proclaim to you: GOD IS LIGHT and no shadow of darkness can exist in him. Consequently, if we were to say that we enjoyed fellowship with him and still went on living in darkness, we should be both telling and living a lie. But if we really are living in the same light in which he eternally exists, then we have true fellowship with each other, and the blood, which his Son shed for us keeps us clean from all sin. If we refuse to admit that we are sinners, then we live in a world of illusion and truth becomes a stranger to us. But if we freely admit that we have sinned, we find God utterly reliable and straightforward – he forgives our sins and makes us thoroughly clean from all that is evil." (1 John 1:1-9)*

Just as the disciples had to speak about Jesus because they had experienced his truth in their lives, I cannot leave this world without expressing to you the truth I find in Jesus.

I have found Jesus to be utterly reliable and straightforward. He loves us and he died so that if we trust in him, we can have a restored relationship with God. Our sins can be forgiven and we can have true fellowship with him. God offers us real life with him. I have lived it. I am experiencing it. Even though I often fail in my ability to be the man I should be, God forgives my failure through the richness of his grace found in his Son, Jesus.

You also can experience this amazing grace. It only requires that you ask Jesus into your heart to take control of your life. In him, we experience forgiveness, strength, comfort and peace. My dying wish is that you, too, experience this joyful freedom of true life in Christ.

Don't screw this up. Don't ignore this opportunity. Everything in heaven and on earth depends on the decision you make. It is a free gift, but it must be accepted. It cannot be ignored. This world is not about you and me. It is all about God, and yet he loves us enough to fix our screw-ups if we are willing to allow Jesus control of our hearts. Please do not ignore him.

To God be the glory!

New Prayer Requests I will write again when I am able and my family will give frequent updates when I am not. Please pray for strength for me and for my family. Please also pray for comfort for my grandchildren as they struggle.

Thank you so much for your love and concern and for all your prayers for Beth, our family and me. May God richly bless you and yours. You will never know this side of heaven what your faithful prayers, loving service, notes, hugs, visits and continuous support have meant to us throughout the three years of this struggle.

July 18, 2006

I am still here. Although I am doing very poorly physically, I do believe I am more alive than the Pittsburgh Pirates.

What Am I Learning? *"Be joyful always; pray continually; give thanks in all circumstances, for this is God's will for you in Christ Jesus." (1 Thessalonians 5:16-18)*

Serious panic was setting in. I had just nebulized, taken a significantly larger than normal dose of morphine, taken a lora-zepam to fool my body into thinking it was breathing better than it was, and now I was trying to relax and breathe easy with my BiPAP. Nothing was working!

How do I keep from panicking now, Father? We are not talking about a minor detail here. We are talking about breathing. And what scripture comes to mind? Why one about thankfulness? Isn't there one on how to breathe in all circumstances? Shouldn't there be some scripture about God creating oxygen for our use and pleasure because he is a good God? Instead, it is a scripture about giving thanks in all cir-cumstances. Isn't that asking a little too much?

I had already put part of the scripture into practice. I was ac-tively praying. But I was having a difficult time with the thankful part. As I prayed on the verge of panic, I began to think about God rather than me.

Of course I need to breathe, and you know that. But may-be I am supposed to leave it all up to you. Lord, you have been trustworthy so far. There are so many things in my life for which I can be grateful, all direct gifts from you.

My mind began to relax.

I do belong to you, Jesus. You paid for me with your own blood on the cross; you own me. Since you own me, you are free to do with me as you please. You really love me. You are not going to do anything that will ultimately harm me, even in death.

Physically I am miserable. If I take enough morphine to handle the pain and smooth out the breathing, I fall asleep in my chair all day long. However, there are significant advantages. When I wake up and realize that the Pirates are down by another five or six runs and it is three innings later, I have not had to see all the bad plays and watch our opponents out-gun us once more. It is like watching sports highlights in reverse – they are really "lowlights" and I am not forced to endure them.

So, God, for what should I thank you? The list could be huge:

I have had the most blessed of lives.

I have climbed the mountains in Colorado.

I have sat with my childhood buddy in the General Manager's box of the Pittsburgh Pirates.

I have soared in my plane and raced in my car.

I have been married to my best friend for 37 years.

I have been blessed with the most awesome, funniest, orneriest kids and have gotten to see tremendous growth in their faith as they and their spouses have had to come to grips with this disease and its impact on our family.

I have watched with awe as our grandchildren have tenderly tried to comfort us as we try to deal with my failing body.

I have had more kindnesses done for me in my lifetime than anyone should ever hope for or expect.

I have had the privilege of spending time with so many of my deep, close, personal friends as we have worked through this challenge.

I have seen God at work touching lives over the last three years.

And despite all my failings, Jesus has changed my heart to love others in ways I never thought possible. For this I am most grateful.

"For if a man is in Christ he becomes a new person altogether – the past is finished and gone, everything has become fresh and new." (2 Corinthians 5:17)

To God be the glory!

August 5, 2006

I do not want to say that I have been taking too much morphine, but I told my son Mike that the Pirates' trade for WWF wrestler King

Kong Bundy and Green Bay quarterback Brett Favre was the worst decision in their history.

I am in the middle of great difficulty with my morphine dosage, trying to balance the need to take it for my breathing and the need to be lucid. People have argued about whether or not I have been lucid for years, but I have to say that I prefer it. It is really hard not to feel in complete control of my faculties.

What Am I Learning? *A week ago Tuesday was a fairly unusual day for the Chilcoat clan. My mother-in-law and brother-in-law were flying in from Florida to visit us for a week. While they were en route, Beth, Andy and my son-in-law Nathan thought I might be dying and that we should go to Kobacker House. Mike and Kimie picked Grandma and Charlie up at the airport and brought them directly to the hospital. They arrived and joined family and friends in various stages of conversation. Because I was having a terrible time breathing, the nurses and doctors were giving me larger and larger doses of morphine. As I groggily tried to process the conversations, I picked up snippets of discussion from around the room:*

"Just try to sleep, Dad. Do you want me to rub your legs?"

"He sure looks out of it. How are you doing, Dad?"

"Another 'surprising' Pirate loss."

"Do you want another laxative?"

"Hi, Grandma and Uncle Charlie!"

"Hey, why is the main ingredient in this automotive anti-freeze?"

"Do cell phones work in here?"

"The Buckeye football team might be number one this year."

"Do you need anything, Dad?"

"Hey, this stuff is like Saturday Night Live's *'Super Colon Blow'!"*

So, I am thinking, 'Are the Buckeyes out of it? The season has not even started! Do the Pirates need a laxative in order to get going? Why would you need antifreeze for a cell phone? Why would Grandma rub Charlie's legs? Just give me the Super Colon Blow!'

Needless to say, I was confused. At times, when things do not make sense, it is hard to know what is really true. And yet, even when I do not understand anything else that is going on around me, there are things I know to be true.

This Truth is something to hold onto at night when I cannot breathe. It is true when I am lying in my bed, fighting fear. It remains true when my pain feels unbearable and my confidence falters. And it is true when I look out the window on a good day and watch my grandchildren throwing softballs in my backyard. It is always true.

What is this Truth that I trust? First, I know scripture is true. It is the Word of God that he uses to lead us.

"Your word is a lamp to my feet, and a light for my path."(Psalm 119:105)

We have to know this Word and when we do, it guides us and is always trustworthy.

Secondly, because I know that scripture is true, I know heaven is true. Salvation through Jesus is true and I will see him.

"I am the way, the truth, and the life." (John 14:6)

"For God so loved the world that he gave his one and only Son, that whoever believes in him shall not perish but have eternal life. For God did not send his Son into the world to condemn the world, but to save the world through him." (John 3:16-17)

Heaven's Truth puts all of life in perspective.

Thirdly, I know God's love for me is true. The Holy Spirit assures me constantly that He loves me. He has shown me in countless ways as he has helped me through this.

"And I pray that you, being rooted and established in love, may have power, together with all the saints, to grasp how wide and long and high and deep is the love of Christ, and to know this love that surpasses knowledge – that you may be filled to the measure of all the fullness of God." (Ephesians 3:17b-19)

He has shown me in the people who drive for hours or even fly in from great distances just to see me. He has shown me by giving me people who stay up all night just to be there and roll me over so I can be comfortable. He has shown me in the people who arrive every day with food. He has shown me by giving me such a wonderful family and friends who surround me with all the care and love that I could possibly hope for or need. He has shown me in the literally thousands of people praying for me. He has shown me when He gives me peace as I lay in bed at night. And He enables me to face even my own death without fear. Through it all, he has shown me his all-encompassing love.

So what can I say? God's own Word says, "And you will know the Truth and the Truth will set you free!" (John 8:32)

And you have.

You have set me free from fear.

You have set me free to know that I will see my family again.

You have set me free to remember that this is not all there is.

You have set me free.

To you, God, be the glory.

Epilogue

David died peacefully at home with his family on August 30, 2006. It sounded quiet here only because we "could not hear the angels singing and the huge party going on in heaven." As we grieve, we also rejoice knowing that he is strong, healthy, free of ALS and celebrating with the Lord. How I will love sharing with him my joy in the publication of his journal. I will have that privilege some day.

A few days before David died, his good friend and personal physician Dr. Bill Wulf came to our home for a last visit. They spoke of his death. Dr. Wulf shared the following account:

"...As a Christian physician, I mark my Christian patients' charts with a cross. This discovery with some patients may take several years. Dave Chilcoat's chart was marked the first visit.

"Dave was born to talk about Christ. He was outgoing, bright and loved to share his faith. In October of 2003, he was seen for his yearly physical. He complained of severe muscle cramping and within the month was diagnosed with ALS. Thus, began this story.

"Over the next three years, Dave and I met regularly for lunch. He loved Asian food and we would meet at his favorite restaurant. As his physician I watched his decline. As a Christian I watched his faith strengthen. In time, Dave's illness progressed and I began taking lunch to his home. I watched as his trust in the Lord never wavered.

"As the end drew near, I wondered if Dave would begin to respond in a more 'human' fashion. The week before he died, I visited Dave and Beth at home. Dave struggled for breath before moving from his wheelchair to his bed. He began to cry. Through tears he said, 'I wish God would give me more time.' I thought to myself, 'Finally, he's responding normally. He's asking for more time for himself at last.' But then Dave said, 'There are just so many more people I want to tell.' This man was at the brink of death, yet still concerned about those who had not yet heard about life in Jesus.

"As a physician, I have watched many patients die of chronic illness. I had the privilege of caring for Dave Chilcoat. Dave not only lived for the Lord, he died for him."

David was truly God's man. His illness and death profoundly affected all of us who loved him. But it is his life, his choice to live and share his faith both before and during the struggle with ALS, that continues to have a far greater impact.

This book is an account of and testimony to God's faithfulness throughout David's life. It is my hope that God will use it to reach even more people with the message David deeply believed – the Gospel of God's love in Jesus Christ – so that even in death, nobody tells this dying guy to shut up.

Beth Chilcoat

Godspeed

Dave and Beth's daughter Jenny, a recording artist and music minister, wrote this song for her father's memorial service. When performing it in concert, she explains, "The first half of these lyrics may be the saddest you've ever heard. They describe the way I was feeling when I lost my Dad. But the second half is the way God answered me when I cried out to Him, reminding me of Jesus' promise of a place with Him on the other side."

Godspeed
John 14:1-6
Music and lyrics by Jennifer Shaw[4]
This song is dedicated to the memory of my dad, David Chilcoat

Goodbye. The world is not a better place.
You've torn an empty, aching space in my heart.
Goodbye. I know that now your pain is done.
Your life in heaven's just begun, but I'm still here.

Sorry for your loss, just give it time.
He's in a better place, yes, but the loss is still mine.
Can you hear those church bells chime?
Marking the march of time, oh, the march of time.

He was a godly man who loved the Lord.
But no matter the strength of his love,
His God loved him more.

And He held him through the storm,
Across to the other shore, oh, the other shore.

But we don't live like the rest of the world –
We know that this is not the end.
So though I'll grieve your loss to my soul,
I know I'll see you again.

So not goodbye.
For those who love the Lord it's true.
He's prepared a place for you, and for me too.
So not goodbye, no, 'cause I'll see you on the other side.
And there your arms will open wide and I'll run in.

I love you.
I'll miss you.
But I'll see you again.
This parting is not forever.
Godspeed, my Friend.

Young Jenny with her dad

[4]*Godspeed* ©2006 Jennifer C. Shaw. www.jennifershawmusic.com

Resources

Catalogue of Scripture References

Prologue

Psalm 23	New International Version	October 28, 2003
Psalm 103	NIV	
Matthew 6:34	J.B. Phillips Translation	
James 1:2-5a	Phillips	

Chapter 1

Matthew 6:34	Phillips	December 27, 2003
John 15:5,11	Phillips	January 31, 2004
James 1:5	Phillips	February 6, 2004
2 Corinthians 12:9	NIV	February 20, 2004

Chapter 2

2 Timothy 2:11-12a	Phillips	March 14, 2004
James 4:7	Dave Chilcoat Version	April 20, 2004
1 Corinthians 10:13	DCV	
Matthew 6:34	Phillips	May 5, 2004
Jeremiah 29:11	NIV	
Psalm 69:1-3a,13-18	NIV	May 12, 2004
Psalm 23:4	NIV	

Chapter 3

Psalm 103:1-5,15-16	NIV	June 24, 2004
1 Corinthians 15:54-55	Phillips	July 3, 2004
Philippians 4:8	Phillips	August 13, 2004
Ephesians 2:1-2	Phillips	

Chapter 4

2 Chronicles 20:17	NIV	September 18, 2004
Psalm 42:1-3	NIV	October 26, 2004
1 Peter 5:5b-7	Phillips	November 5, 2004
James 1:12	Phillips	
2 Corinthians 5:1	Phillips	November 13, 2004

Chapter 5

Genesis 2:24	NIV	February 5, 2005
Matthew 22:37-39	Phillips	
Proverbs 31:10-12,25-31	NIV	
Matthew 11:28-30	Phillips	February 23, 2005

Chapter 6

Romans 5:2b-5	NIV	March 6, 2005
Judges 6:1-7:22	NIV	April 9, 2005
1 Corinthians 1:27-31	NIV	
Hebrews 13:8	NIV	
2 Thessalonians 3:3	Phillips	
Romans 8:13	Phillips	

Chapter 7

Psalm 142:1-3a	NIV	July 20, 2005
2 Corinthians 12:9-10	NIV	
Psalm 142:5-7a	NIV	
Psalm 146	NIV	
Joshua 24:15	NIV	August 13, 2005

Chapter 8

Hebrews 11:1	NIV	October 28, 2005
1 Corinthians 3:18-19	Phillips	

Chapter 9

1 Corinthians 15:55-57	Phillips	December 28, 2005
Jude 24-25	Phillips	February 9, 2006
John 14:1-3	Phillips	February 25, 2006
Revelation 7:16-17	Phillips	

Chapter 10

Psalm 31:9-10	NIV	March 14, 2006
Psalm 31:1-2	NIV	
Matthew 14:22-32	Phillips	
Ephesians 5:31	NIV	April 1, 2006
Revelation 21:4	NIV	May 15, 2006

Chapter 11

Psalm 4:1,8	NIV	June 29, 2006
Hebrews 13:5b	NIV	July 8, 2006
1 John 1:1-9	Phillips	
1 Thessalonians 5:16-18	NIV	July 18, 2006
2 Corinthians 5:17	Phillips	
Psalm 119:105	NIV	August 5, 2006
John 14:6	NIV	
John 3:16-17	NIV	
Ephesians 3:17b-19	NIV	
John 8:32	Phillips	

What Am I Learning from Dave's Relationships?
A Guide for Your Reflection

Dave shows us how to live and die into the love and hope of eternal life with God and with those who love Him. This guide is framed around his relationships with God, with Beth and their family, with his friends and with himself.

Like personal Psalms, Dave regularly shared his feelings – joy, fear, faith, suffering. They were part of his nighttime conversations with Jesus. He called those portions of his online journal *What Am I Learning?*

What are you learning?

Take advantage of his Psalms and the questions they stirred in your soul. Feel free to begin a journal of your own in the following pages by responding to questions and adding your own.

Relationship with God

Dave clearly enjoyed an intimate relationship with God. How did it begin? Have you ever made that same decision?

Dave and God talked often. Their conversations included Dave's requests, praise, honest complaints, fears, frustration and gratitude. Which aspects of these prayers do you experience? Are there any that surprise you? How might you expand your prayer life?

Dave knew and loved the Bible, God's written word. How did God use His word to strengthen Dave?

Dave was confident in God's goodness in spite of the disease (see *What Am I Learning*, December 28, 2005; May 15, 2006 and February 09, 2006). What can you learn from Dave's confidence?

How did his confidence in heaven affect the way he lived on earth?

How did he not ruin the days he had with worry about his future?

Relationship among Dave, Beth and family

Dave enjoyed an intimate relationship with Beth and his family. What attitudes in regard to marriage did he exhibit that might strengthen your marriage or relationships?

Dave states that his marriage with Beth was strengthened during their years of ALS. How do you think that happened?

What role did Dave and Beth's commitment to serve one another play in that process (see *What Am I Learning*, April 1, 2006)?

Which of your relationships would be strengthened if you committed to serve sacrificially?

Relationships with Christian friends:

Dave was surrounded by many close friendships based on shared Christian faith. How do you think such strong relationships developed?

Excluding the universal excuse of lack of time, what barriers prevent you from experiencing all the benefits of close friendships?

It is never too late to begin to build strong relationships. How could you begin such relationships? How could you deepen the friendships you have?

Relationship to himself:

How do you see the value of Dave's using his memory to recall Bible passages and promises?

How could Dave have chosen praise, and humor and hope in the midst of much fear, loss and pain? Where does hope beyond death come from? What is the reason for hope that is stronger than death?

How, and where in the story, do you see the value of Dave's humility to receive? What would have happened if he had become proud? What are some of the reasons for, and benefits of, humility?

What Am I Learning?

Discussion Questions by Chapter for Further Reflection

Chapter 1 – Winter: We Still Have a Life

What could you learn from Dave about reacting to unwelcome news (Prologue)?

As Dave prayed about his disease, in what ways did God answer him? Can you see unexpected ways in which God is answering your prayers (February 6, 2004)?

How did Dave avoid bitterness and find joy? How do the miracles he wrote of differ from the miracle of healing? Were they really miracles (February 20, 2004)?

Chapter 2 – Spring: Coming into Deep Waters

Dave refers to "friends he has known and loved for forty years." What was the basis for his relationships that grew so deep? What part does fellowship play in your life (May 5, 2004; March 5, 2006)?

How was Dave able to keep worry over the future from stealing his joy in the present? How might you apply this to your own life (May 5, 2006)?

What was your reaction to Dave's claim that he came into a relationship with God as a result of one decision (March 14, 2004)?

Chapter 3 – Summer: Reaching for the Higher Things

Are you 100% confident of the truth of heaven? How should this assurance change the way you live here on earth (July 3, 2004)?

When struggling, how did Dave use Scripture to restore his joy and peace? How could you begin to use praise and thanksgiving in your circumstances? Are you living in the future or thankfully enjoying the present (June 24, 2004)?

Chapter 4 – Fall: Lessons from the First Year

As you reflect on your life, how have you seen God at work changing and growing you? Is your life better described as the airplane on the ground following your own plans or as the plane soaring in God's plans (November 5, 2004)?

Have you ever fully surrendered your life plans to God? What things are you holding onto that God wants you to release to Him (November 5, 2004)?

Chapter 5 – Winter: It Is Well with My Soul

What attitudes in regard to marriage did Dave mention that might strengthen your marriage or relationships (February 5, 2005)?

In what ways has God altered your plans over the years? How has He used them for good (February 23, 2005)?

Chapter 6 – Spring: God Remains the Same

In light of Dave's Young Life talk, what have you learned about God's character? How could this affect the way you view future trials (April 9, 2005)?

How do struggles and hardships in your life open up opportunities to minister to others (May 13, 2005)?

Dave experienced a number of different calls on his life over the years. Where might God be calling you to step out in faith now (April 9, 2005)?

Chapter 7 – Summer: Stop Long Enough to Look

Dave wrestles with not being able to do much. Is your self-image dependent on what you do or who you are (July 20, 2005)?

What things testify most to you of God's hand in creation (August 5, 2005)?

When do you find it hardest to choose God (August 13, 2005)?

Chapter 8 – Fall: Fixing My Eyes on the Unseen

How did Dave experience the reality of God, even when he could not see God? What does he mean by "setting our instruments to receive his leading, and watching for signs" (October 28, 2005)?

What did you learn about choosing thankfulness (November 23, 2005)?

Chapter 9 – Winter: Daunting Circumstances and Dearest Gifts

Is your confidence in God's goodness dependent on receiving specific blessings or answers to prayer? What can you learn from Dave's confidence in God's goodness (December 28, 2005; February 9, 2006)?

What Bible verses help you picture the reality of heaven (February 25, 2006)?

Chapter 10 – Spring: Hope Stronger than My Distress

How does serving someone strengthen the love in that relationship (April 1, 2006)?

What aspects of Dave's relationships with family or friends were most appealing to you? Within the Biblical framework, any picture of human relationships is a glimpse of the intimate love relationship God desires with us through Christ. What new insights into God's love did you get through Dave's writings about his marriage, family or friends (April 1, 2006)?

How did Dave show his trust in God's sovereignty in times of despair (May 15, 2006)?

Chapter 11 – Summer: I Am Free!

What names do you fear God might call you? What names does He truly call you? Have you chosen to receive God as your Lord? What difference does that decision make in who you are in God's eyes (June 11, 2006)?

Why is it important to Dave that nobody tells a dying guy to shut up? How is God using you to share the gospel (July 8, 2006)?

What did you learn from Dave about how he faces his fears (July 8, 2006)?

In what ways is Dave set free (August 5, 2006)? In what ways could God free you?

What Am I Learning?
Personal Reflections

Internet Resources

www.bethchilcoat.com for more on *Nobody Tells a Dying Guy to Shut Up.*

www.davechilcoat.com for Dave's complete online journal

www.youtube.com/watch?v=FDaNe665rCc to see Dave's video, "God's Man"

www.younglife.org to learn more about Young Life

www.alsa.org for more information on Amyotrophic Lateral Sclerosis (ALS), or "Lou Gehrig's disease"

www.jennifershawmusic.com to hear the music of Dave and Beth's daughter Jennifer

The Best and Worst of Times
Pittsburgh Sports
(Winter 2003 – Summer 2006)

The Pittsburgh Pirates

Year	Total Games	Games Won-Lost	Division Standing	Manager
2004	161	72-89	5th of 6	Lloyd McClendon
2005	162	67-95	6th of 6	Lloyd McClendon replaced by Pete Mackanin
2006	162	67-95	5th of 6	Jim Tracy

The Pittsburgh Steelers 2003
Bill Cowher, Head Coach

W-6, L-10		Steelers	Opp.	
09/07	Baltimore	34	15	(W)
09/14	@Kansas City	20	41	(L)
09/21	@Cincinnati	17	10	(W)
09/28	Tennessee	13	30	(L)
10/05	Cleveland	13	33	(L)
10/12	@Denver	14	17	(L)
10/19	Idle			
10/26	St. Louis*	21	33	(L)
11/02	@Seattle	16	23	(L)
11/09	Arizona	28	15	(W)
11/17	@San Francisco	14	30	(L)
11/23	@Cleveland	13	06	(W)
11/30	Cincinnati	20	24	(L)
12/07	Oakland	27	07	(W)
12/14	@New York Jets	00	08	(L)
12/21	San Diego	40	24	(W)
12/28	@Baltimore	10	13	(L/OT)
(H 4-4, A 2-6)		**300**	**327**	

*1,000th Game in Steelers History

The Pittsburgh Steelers 2004

Bill Cowher, Head Coach

W-15, L-1		Steelers	Opp.	
09/12	Oakland	24	21	(W)
09/19	@Baltimore	13	30	(L)
09/26	@Miami	13	03	(L)
10/03	Cincinnati	28	17	(W)
10/10	Cleveland	34	23	(W)
10/17	@Dallas	24	20	(W)
10/24	Idle			
10/31	New England	34	20	(W)
11/07	Philadelphia	27	03	(W)
11/14	@Cleveland	24	10	(W)
11/21	@Cincinnati	19	14	(W)
11/28	Washington	16	07	(W)
12/05	@Jacksonville	17	16	(W)
12/12	New York Jets	17	06	(W)
12/18	@NY Giants	33	30	(W)
12/26	Baltimore	20	07	(W)
01/02	@Buffalo	29	24	(W)
(H 8-0, A 7-1)		**372**	**251**	

AFC Playoff Game (Divisional)

01/15	New York Jets	20	17	(W/OT)

AFC Championship Game

01/23	New England	27	31	(L)

The Pittsburgh Steelers 2005

Bill Cowher, Head Coach

W-11, L-5		Steelers	Opp.	
09/11	Tennessee	34	07	(W)
09/18	@Houston	27	07	(W)
09/25	New England	20	23	(L)
10/02	Idle			
10/10	@San Diego	24	22	(W)
10/16	Jacksonville	17	23	(L)
10/23	@Cincinnati	27	13	(W)
10/31	Baltimore	20	19	(W)
11/06	@Green Bay	20	10	(W)
11/13	Cleveland	34	21	(W)
11/20	@Baltimore	13	19	(L)
11/28	@Indianapolis	07	26	(L)
12/04	Cincinnati	31	38	(L)
12/11	Chicago	21	09	(W)
12/18	@Minnesota	18	03	(W)
12/24	@Cleveland	41	00	(W)
01/01	Detroit	35	21	(W)
(H 5-3, A 6-2)		**389**	**258**